ONCE UPON A TIME

On the Nature of Fairy Tales

Max Lüthi

*Translated by Lee Chadeayne and Paul Gottwald
with additions by the author*

*Introduction and reference notes
by Francis Lee Utley*

FREDERICK UNGAR PUBLISHING CO.
NEW YORK

Translated from the German
Es war einmal
by arrangement with the original publishers,
Verlag Vandenhoeck & Ruprecht.
© Vandenhoek & Ruprecht, Gottingen

Copyright © 1970 by Frederick Ungar Publishing Co., Inc.
Printed in the United States of America
Library of Congress Catalog Card Number 79-118-870
ISBN 0-8044-2565-5

TRANSLATOR'S NOTE

This translation of Lüthi's *Es war einmal . . . vom Wesen des Volks-märchens* includes some additions suggested by the author, especially the material comprising Chapter 4, taken from a series of newspaper articles that appeared in the Winterthur *Sonntagspost*.

In order to make some English equivalents available to the reader, the bibliographical reference notes have been expanded for this edition by Francis Lee Utley.

L. C.

CONTENTS

INTRODUCTION

Americans love fairy tales as much as the Germans and the Swiss
do—as much, indeed, as all men do. Our classic watershed in fiction lies between romance and the novel; any culture with Haw-
thorne, Melville, Irving, Poe, Chase, Randolph, and Barth need
not humble itself below that of the lands of Hoffmann, Kleist,
Hauff, Jacob and Wilhelm Grimm, Novalis, Bechstein, Haiding,
and Kafka. Although we sometimes remark today that fairy tales,
once broad in appeal, are no longer for grownups, we flock to buy
the works of the Englishman William Golding, to learn not only
about our inner fantasies but also about our outer realities.

When it comes to serious study, it is true that only a relatively few American scholars have discovered the poetry and the
truth of the folk tale; measured against Scandinavia, Ireland,
Germany, and Finland, our study of the history and meaning of
the folk tale has been minimal. Yet our study of English and
Scottish and American popular ballads has outstripped the
mother country, and our anthropology, particularly of American
Indian and African cultures, leads the world. Even for the folk tale,

our organizing ability, manifest especially in the energetic hands of Stith Thompson, has provided the basic indexes of type and motif for an international audience. Thompson's initial impulse, however, came from Finland and Sweden; the core of his work came from the archives of Europe which specialize in folk narrative.

Since comparative folklorists find such indexes of special help, the most competent elder generation of scholars, such as Thompson and Archer Taylor, were closely committed to the principles of the "Finnish school," the historical-geographical method. Its purpose was to avoid the broad generalizations which led a great scholar like Theodor Benfey, in the nineteenth century, to derive (or seem to derive, since polemics always tends toward exaggeration) most folk tales from the Indian *Panchatantra*. He was aided by the French student of Lorraine tales, Emmanuel Cosquin, who like many disciples, went the master one better. In place of such reductive pictures of folk-tale history, the Finnish school offered the positive new challenge of a series of studies of each folk-tale type or entity, the combined versions of "Cinderella," "Sleeping Beauty," "Rapunzel," "The Dragon Slayer," and "The Clever Peasant Girl." All versions, collected throughout the world from oral sources, were to be brought together, filed and analyzed, and the result was to be the life history of a folk tale. If done well, this work would ultimately be combined into the true history of the migration of folk tales the world over.

Within limits, remarkable results can be, and have been, obtained. Casual views which assumed that folk-tale study was a set of hit-or-miss evidence and hypothetical lost versions, of mysterious and vaguely related combinations of chains of loosely connected tales, of common sources and communal composition in the Germanic forests, or archetypes and urtypes and confused subtypes—all of this magic mist has been replaced with the use of identifiable documents and clearly traceable process, with positive light and truth. If one studies, as William Bettridge has done, sixty extant tales of Type 887, Griselda, one finds that all the folk-tale examples (as well as the many literary examples) unquestionably derive from Boccaccio, Petrarch, and Chaucer. Though the entity is clearly oral in one of its manifestations, the

oral end product is clearly the result of chapbook, or "cheap
book," intermediaries. There is an even more striking conclusion.
The modern oral versions are found in Scandinavia, Germany,
Ireland, and a few outlying posts; they are wholly absent from
Italy and the Mediterranean lands, which theoretically should
have provided the sources for Boccaccio's version of about 1350,
as well as ample reflections of Boccaccio in present tradition. I
have seen many casual references about the popularity of
Griselda in humble peasant pictures and in puppet shows; this
may be true. But not one record of an oral version of Type 887 is
present in modern Italy, whereas the tale is beloved in northern
Europe. Such is a positive, well-supported result of this kind of
folk-tale study.

Similarly, Jan-Öyvind Swahn, gathering and tabulating a
thousand examples of the so-called "Cupid and Psyche legend,"
places that tale on a sounder footing. We find that the famous
version in Apuleius's *Golden Ass,* which gives its name to the
elaborate complex of versions, is anything but typical, and it is
certainly not the archetype from which they all derive. These two
folk tales demonstrate the ambivalent nature of our evidence and
the risk of simplistic theory. One modern oral tale, Griselda,
derives from a medieval literary version; another prolific oral tale,
Cupid and Psyche (better called "the monster bridegroom"),
existed long enough ago to give rise to a famous ancient literary
version long thought to be its ancestor. Thus, the folk tale can
both create and borrow. With such clear evidence for both the
proletarian and the aristocratic views of folk-tale origin, we see
that each is only a half truth. There is something in *"das Volk
dichtet"* and in *"gesunkenes Kulturgut,"* as well, but neither is a
complete theory of folk-tale composition or process.

Many such life histories of single-tale types have been worked
out, most of them in German, the second language encouraged by
the scholars who worked with the Finnish Literary Society, which
sponsored the method in the early years of the twentieth century.
Because of the language barrier, few of these life histories have
been available to beginning students in America. Most teachers
of the folk tale despair of demonstrating this method in the class-

room, because the implements are linguistically, technically, out
of reach. For students, the best technical exercise is a term paper,
and these are scarcely possible when the task is to collect a thousand versions from forty foreign archives, not to speak of many
out-of-the-way printed books. At most, one can work with twenty
or thirty versions in a brief college quarter or semester.

It is not surprising, then, that many of the younger and more
serious American students of the folk tale, like Roger Abrahams,
Alan Dundes, and Butler Waugh, have rebelled somewhat con-
spicuously from the Finnish method. Their eyes have been open
to new challenges: psychological studies with depth to them, sociological studies with breadth to them, so-called "structural"
studies which heed the configurational bias of the twentieth
century rather than the genetic and historical bias of the nineteenth. To those who have arduously trained themselves in the
older techniques, it sometimes seems that these new men have
cavalierly abandoned one important sector of the science. We
forget that they, like all sound scholars, will come back to that
sector when they need it again. And they are genuinely aware of
the problem of student time. Whether the new techniques are
always more relevant than the historical is not always clear; but
that they are more easily practiced in a country without major
folk tale archives, liftetime appointments to research institutes,
and early university specialization in scholarly discipline, is clear
enough.

One error has been to assume that continental scholarship,
which does have the archives, the appointments, and the discipline, has been remiss in other areas than the historical and
geographical ones. The sociological approach of Roger Abrahams
is matched by the work of Lutz Röhrich of Marburg, by Linda
Dégh of Budapest (now of Indiana), and the Hungarian and
Russian ethnographers. Their comprehension of the social nature
of the folk tale is, if anything, broader than any displayed in this
country.

Depth psychology, the interpretation of the single tale in
terms of some kind of Jungian or Freudian archetype, is a favorite new method, often practiced in a mechanical manner and

without paying attention to the significance of the individual teller. "Psychological universals" like the great mother, the Oedipal drive, and the Cainite urge, submerge the individual psyche. And yet the human being who tells the story is quite as important to any ultimate hypothesis of archetype as a single folk-tale history is to the history of the genre. More so, indeed, if depth psychology is really interested in its proper subject matter, the living person. Whatever we may print, we need in our files not only the record of the tale, but a conversation of the teller with the recorder which reveals something about his personality and the biases it may give to the way he tells the tale. It is not enough to take one tale with a mother bias; we need to compare it with another where the tone is more masculine, even though the tale type is identical. None will deny that we owe a major debt to Vienna and to Zürich in spurring us toward such problems. Few realize how far the European study of the traces of the subliminal in folk tales has gone. We may not agree with all of Hedwig von Beit's conclusions in her massive three-volume study, *The Symbolism of Fairy Tales* (for full citation, see Reference Notes), but we had better read her before we decide that our new attempts are original and unique or not. America does have its Jungian study of myth, Joseph Campbell's recent *The Masks of God*, but its province is less that of the oral tale and more that of learned tradition.

Young American structuralists like Alan Dundes frankly acknowledge their debts to the Russian formalist Vladimir Propp and the French anthropologist Lévi-Strauss. Though we may have our reservations about Propp's tendency to reduce the folk tale to a few polarities, reminiscent of Roman Jakobson's linguistic binaries, we have to admit he knows his folk tales—he is the editor of the best modern version of Afanasiev's classic Russian collection. Lévi-Strauss is a redoubtable anthropologist, with countless cultures in his hands, ready to be molded to his models. Europe is once more the master of method in the folk tale, as America has long been in the ballad under the impetus of Francis James Child, who gave as much to the Danish Svend Grundtvig as he got from him. Our American claim for theoretical novelty, perhaps a pro-

jection of our feelings of inadequacy when we look at our local
archival material, reminds us of one of the ironies unconsciously
reflected by those who, a quarter of a century ago, attacked the
German Ph.D. in philology. Imported in the late nineteenth
century by Johns Hopkins, it has been perennially assaulted by
reformers; the latest assault has been from one of the brightest
stars in Hopkins's own constellation, Don Cameron Allen. In the
early 1930s, this attack was carried on largely by Irving Babbitt
and the New Humanists, joined by the embryo New Critics, inspired by John Crowe Ransom. Babbitt stuck to his guns; he
consistently preferred Sainte-Beuve and Joubert (did you ever
hear of him?) and Arnold to ten Brinks and Herders and
Grimms and even Goethes, who were too affirmative for him. But
the younger critics made a strange substitution for the Teutonic
has-beens who were wrecking our criticism: they gave us instead
Freud and Jung and Marx and Weber and Cassirer and Tillich
and Niebuhr and Frobenius and Curtius and Rilke and Mann,
and now, somewhat belatedly, Hermann Hesse.

The enemy, in short, was not Germany (including Switzerland and Austria), which provided vital new ideas somewhat in
advance of our own. Their rebellion preceded ours, just as the
glorious revolution of 1688 preceded that of 1776. German study
of the folk tale, or of anything else, can, we may admit, be so
steeped in theoretical constructs that it loses sight of the splendid
artifacts of literature, oral and written. Sometimes abstractions
and summaries and symbols replace the living word and the
living drama. Once I got into serious trouble with a distinguished
anthropologist of the Frobenius branch of the *Kulturkreis* school,
when I said that every German writer had to begin with ten pages
in which he set himself right with Immanuel Kant. Adolf Jenson,
who did not find this funny, insisted that he was no Kantian.
That wasn't the point, of course. I made up the remark because I
wanted to encourage my students to read beyond the tenth page,
when the data and the real point of the book would begin to
emerge, and when the style would smoothe out and abandon
antinomies and the categorical imperative (or the Hegelian thesis,
antithesis, and synthesis, if you prefer). What I was really trying

to do was to get them to read German; to urge them to make use of the excited new ideas and exciting new data which a book by von der Leyen or Bolte and Polívka or Röhrich or Jolles or Dégh could provide. I thought that if they skipped the ten pages of philosophizing, they might more quickly get down to business.

We have been speaking about continental and German antecedents of our own embryonic efforts in sociological, psychological, and structural study of the folk tale. Almost nonexistent in this country is a departure which makes use of all of these, and of historical principles as well—the approach to the folk tale simply as a work of art. Without method behind it, it would be mere impressionism, a romantic heritage far worse than impressionistic literary criticism, because the data is much more tricky and less well known. With the long tradition of serious study of the folk tale since the Grimm brothers, such a fairly recent departure can be a matter of high interest to us all, whether we are serious scholars or beginning students. In either case, we are in search of methods for talking about folk tales intelligently within the limits of our time and our experience. One of the best practitioners of such an approach is Max Lüthi, whose book we are about to read.

II

Max Lüthi was born in 1909 in Bern, Switzerland. He studied history, Germanics, English, and religion at his home university, with an excursion in 1931–1932 to the University of Berlin. In 1936 he began teaching at the Zürich High School for Girls, with specialized fields of German and social studies. Married in 1937 to Miss Toni Treppenhauer, he took his doctorate with honors in medieval Germanic language and literature and modern German literature, as well as in Swiss history, once more at Bern.

As a writer, his work has been mainly in English literature and in European folk narrative. His dissertation was *Die Gabe im Märchen und in der Sage* (The Gift in Fairy Tale and Local Legend), 1943; he had already converted his broad series of specialties into a composite field of folklore. In 1947 appeared his important study, *Des europäische Volksmärchen, Form und Wesen* (The European Folk Tale: Form and Nature); it reached its third edition by 1968. There were a collection of folk tales in 1951, a study of *Rapunzel* in 1958; *Volksmärchen und Volkssage* (Fairy Tale and Legend) in 1961 and 1966; a valuable handbook for beginners called *Märchen* (1962, 1968); and the present book, *Es war einmal . . . vom Wesen des Volksmärchens,* published in Göttingen in 1962 and in a third edition in 1968. Lüthi has also published two important books on Shakespeare: *Shakespeares Dramen* (1957, 1966) and *Shakespeare, Dichter des Wirklichen und des Nichtwirklichen* (Shakespeare, Poet of the Real and the Fantastic) in 1964. The second book applies to high art some of the polar contrasts Lüthi has illuminated in the folk tale. Among his shorter pieces are studies of Swiss and German culture, folklore, and philology, the place of the folk tale in the study of literature, stability and flexibility in the fairy tale, and Shakespeare's ironies. One title, *"Selbstverlust und Selbstver-wirklichung bei Shakespeare"* (Self-Alienation and Self-Realization in Shakespeare), holds out counsel to the people of Haight-Ashbury and Telegraph Avenue. At Athens, in 1965, at the Congress of the International Society for Folk Narrative Research, I heard his significant paper on "Parallel Themes in Folk Tale and *Hochliteratur"* (I leave the lucid German word as it is because we lack its exact equivalent); this was translated and published in *The Journal of the Folklore Institute* in 1967. *"Ahistorische Stile"* (A-Historic Style), dated 1965, opens up a wide range of meaning for us, with the folk tale, as usual, illuminating the written narrative. *"Gebrechliche und Behinderte im Volksmärchen"* (The Weak and the Handicapped in the Folk Tale), in 1966, continues the theme of psychological alienation and its cure; *"Gründe der Faszinationskraft Shakespeares"* (The Basis of Shakespeare's Magic Power), in 1967, shows how a great artist can recapture the folk-tale power we no longer have.

The stream of major publications led to a partial appointment as lecturer at the University of Zürich in 1962 and to a full professorship in European Folk Literature in 1968. Only recently has Lühi begun to be known outside his own country for his wit and breadth and skill in language teaching; he taught at Bread Loaf School in Middlebury, Vermont, in 1967. The present book is the product of a series of radio broadcasts; a sequel was published in 1969, *So leben sie noch heute* (And So They Still Live Today).

In the present book, Lüthi is a practitioner of the best kind of popularization, what the French call *haute vulgarisation,* a term we need more of, just as we do of the German *Hochliteratur.* We could better use the term if we were not put off the scent with the special English connotations of "vulgar." We forget that the Bible could circulate as the Vulgate without losing its sanctity, and that the people's language could be Vulgar Latin (until modern linguists, for reasons irrelevant here, decided to call it "proto-romance") without implying that it was necessarily obscene. Henry James, deeply trained in French culture, used the term "vulgar" too often for American democrats; they failed to realize that his use of the term meant the same as their use of "popular" (later "middlebrow") without any essential connotation of eating peas with a knife or using excrement or custard pies as weapons in an argument.

As our National Endowment for the Humanities has insisted, no doubt with Congress in mind, there is vast room for the popularization of scholarly knowledge. One may wonder why such popularization needs government subsidy, since any publisher worth his salt is anxious to sign up any competent work of the kind, at once, unsolicited. The French term confirms a major truth, that popularization is not of much account if it has nothing significant to popularize. New popular books are of interest because they are based on rapidly moving events on the serious intellectual front, the front which really needs the subsidy. Einstein and Fermi had to be popularized because, as physicists and mathematicians, they spoke in a technical language, absolutely essential for their purposes, but in need of partial translation for the intelligent but nonspecialized reader. Rachel Carson based her *The Sea Around Us* on years of obscure work by marine biologists and ecologists; Paul De Kruif's *Microbe*

Hunters, which inspired Sinclair Lewis's *Arrowsmith,* has all of previrus bacteriology and its organizational and individual head-aches behind it; Whitehead and Russell's popular books on mathematics would have been nothing without their abstruse *Principia Mathematica.*

Yet for some reason, in this country it is assumed that those who write about literature and folk literature must produce the popularization before they produce the *Wissenschaft.* In Germany, Austria, and Switzerland, this is not true. Behind Lüthi's *Once Upon a Time* is not only his own research, but all the serious books on folklore which go back to the Grimms themselves. At last report, there were seventeen chairs of folklore in Germany, and Lüthi has just obtained one at Zurich. Old, solid, and re-spectable universities see to it that the priceless heritage of oral tradition receives the same study as that of Homer, Vergil, Milton, Shakespeare, and Goethe. Of course, Rilke and Günter Grass are not neglected, but one suspects that the immediately fashion-able may not take over the classroom quite so fast in some conti-nental countries as it has threatened to do on this side of the Atlantic. There is some advantage in not attempting to be perpetually Edenic.

III

With a secure base in the knowledge of high literature and folk narrative, as practiced both by others and by himself, Lüthi has been able to move to the folk-tale entity with ease and with imagination, and to provide us with a model for the criticism of that neglected genre. His ten lectures on folk tale and legend (which the translators have swelled by one intercalary chapter on Cinderella, Hansel and Gretel, and the white snake, taken from Lüthi's independent essays), are each a systematic assault on major problems of the meaning and use of the folk tale.

In his first chapter, on *Dornröschen,* or Sleeping Beauty, he discusses the relationship between form and content in the fairy tale. Though he is both a scientist and a structuralist, he has not

lost his sense of poetry. Like Mark Schorer, he can discover
meaning through technique. Aware of the mysticism in the
Grimms' discussion of the survival of myth in the folk tale, he
treats it as metaphor and not as science, as broad human meaning
rather than the mere local cult and ritual which the Cambridge
anthropologists tried to make it. The fairy tale is wise, lucid,
realistic in the midst of fantasy. Its structure is outlined by dramatic climaxes, a ladder of gifts leading to the neglected and
malignant fairy at the top, a palace sinking into sleep and re-
awakening as the princess awakes. Strict folklorists (and the
younger they are, the stricter they are) discover time and again,
with alarm, that the Grimms touched up, or "literated," their
informants' tales. They excommunicate the pioneers of their
science, just as they make it hard for that master of American folk-
tale and ballad collecting, Vance Randolph (he has never, for
instance, had a Guggenheim Fellowship). Lüthi shows us the art
of how the drama is sharpened and how the irony, destructive of
sentiment, is deepened; he refuses to denigrate either the art of
the Grimms or the fine simplicity of the folk which gave them
their cue. Both are seen as part of the same clearly delineated
process. The critique includes the historical dimension of period
contrast: romantic Grimms against baroque Basile. We discover
the structural element of organic repetition: "the flax fiber which
puts Talia to sleep plays a role again in her awakening." And
since the flax fiber is sucked out of the sleeping mother's finger,
our allegiances to the subliminal depth of the psyche are satisfied;
we achieve one more dimension and a more profound emotional
correlative. This repetition of structural detail is exactly like the
boast of old January in Chaucer's *Merchant's Tale.* When he
takes young May as wife, he says he can mold her like warm wax;
she ironically uses warm wax to take the impression of the key to
the garden in which she is to meet her love, and, metaphorically,
she molds his opinions like warm wax at the end of the tale, when
she convinces him that he has not seen it "like it is." Thus, structure and visual objective correlative works for a medieval artist
just as it does for the Grimm tale.

By showing us the special style of a Perrault version of the same story, Lüthi adds the dimension of formal stylistics. Perrault, keenly aware of his courtly audience, fills the prince with the same kind of embarrassed sensibility as Troilus showed to Cressida in his first real meeting with her. As Lüthi puts it, "Little eloquence, much love." The princess is dressed like the prince's grandmother, and the chamber music is 100 years out of date. Here, we are far from the folk, whose leisure leaves them little time to consider fashions, either in dress or in music. How much more central these observations than those of old, which identified the wicked fairy with the "neglected" thirteenth month and made a lunar hypothesis out of the tale!

In his second chapter, Lüthi takes up the legend of "The Seven Sleepers," which brings genre criticism in its train. A literary critic, however awkwardly he defines it, knows the difference between poetry and prose; a folklorist, the difference between complex fairy tale and simple local legend (*Märchen* or *Sage*). The fairy tale "Cinderella" is diffused from Ireland to India, or vice versa; the local legend will crop up all over one country or be confined to a small area, but its further migration is unusual. The fairy tale is fiction; the local legend, however miraculous its ties to the spirit world, is in some measure counted on as true, as straight, or as wondrous history worth retelling. A third category is the saint's legend (*Legende*). It combines fiction with history, but above all, it is learned in origin and transmission, and its end is not information but religious edification. Like all literary genres, these three merge into one another at the edges; but the first step in understanding is taken by recognizing the categories, as Aristotle taught us long ago. "Sleeping Beauty" is a fairy tale; "The Seven Sleepers" and Grimm's "The Twelve Apostles" are saints' legends; the tale of Prior Evo from the canton of Wallis in Switzerland is a local legend. All four contain the common motif of awakening after a long sleep, but they differ in style and form and tone. There is realism and a mood of dust and ashes about the story of Prior Evo which is absent in "Sleeping Beauty," and a special mood of edification in the two saints' legends absent from the others. Americans will recall that one famous legend which we associate with our Catskills, "Rip Van Winkle," is both local and migratory. Washington Irving's local color is impeccable and his national purpose, the bridging of the gap between a land where George III and one where George Washington was honored, incontestable. Yet it is a bald borrowing of a German *Volkssage,* Johann Carl Cristoph Nachtigall's "Peter Klaus the Goatherd," associated with the Kyffhäuser just southeast of the Hartz Mountains in Saxony. With German help, the American Eden knew a long sleep just at the time of its own awakening.

Turning to another fairy tale, "Dragon Slayer," Lüthi probes more deeply into style: repetition, flat absence of descriptive detail, precision, and clarity of conception, episodes with two actors, the neat polarization which structural critics have extracted as the essence of the folk tale. Episodes are tripled, form is rigidified, and scenes isolated (as in the ballad's famous technique of "leaping and lingering"); the tempo is retarded for suspense and speeded up for action; the whole tale betrays a feeling for "the sacral, the stylized, and the abstract." Hence, the fairy tale is not *as* convincing as realistic fiction, it is *more* convincing. It has no "if" and no "perhaps"; it is the very antithesis of scholarly caution. That is why it is immediate for us and meaningful. We need not explain "Dragon Slayer" by psychological archetypes, by the phallicism of the delousing episodes, or by the equation between the slain dragon and Oedipus's father. We need not call upon these explanatory devices, unless we very much want to do so. If we do, as Kittredge used to say, thought is free. We need not even make the historical gambit, and compare "Dragon Slayer," quite justly, to the ancient Egyptian "Two Brothers", to *Beowulf,* the *Odyssey,* and the *Grettissaga.* There can be ample satisfaction in discovering with Lüthi the simple art of the tale, its style and its structure.

Yet that, like all single views of a literary masterpiece, is but one stage on the way to comprehension. The fairy tale, so rich in art and in the resultant entertainment value, is not without its uses. In the intercalary Chapter 4, inserted by the translators, Lüthi discusses the well-known tales "Cinderella," "Hansel and Gretel," and "The White Snake." "Cinderella" is an initiation, "an imaginative introduction for the listener into the real nature

of his existence," an aid to "finding oneself," of which there is so
much talk today. Though the poetic justice which pursues the
wicked stepsisters in the Grimm version is harsh, it may be a
useful antidote to the sentimental modern view, which en-
courages you to live with almost anything you find. What the
envious girls found was not good; the punishment fits the crime.
Lüthi shows us, however, that the various endings differ, and that
other ages than our own have also been permissive. And in
"Hansel and Gretel," we find an enterprising pair of children who
have already found themselves. They survive without parental
protection and attack the wicked witch on their own, quite as if
she were a projection of their own unconscious view of the power
structure they desire to control. We are apt to be sympathetic with
children who know themselves and their desires so well. The projection goes further in "The White Snake." Here, the power of
the hero to learn the language of the animals is not merely within
himself and the human circle; it produces power over the universe. "A well-known and basic theme finds expression here: man
knows everything better than he knows himself." The animal
helpers help him in his problem-solving, and there is an unobtru-
sive moral. The youth did not gain knowledge because he was
greedy for power, he gained it because he was kind and chari-
table. The tale sets itself valiantly against Joe DiMaggio's despairing cry that the cards are stacked against the good guy.

    The next chapter, The Little Earth-Cow (an American ver-
sion is The Little Red Bull), touchés upon the symbolism which
we should expect of anyone who lives close to the school of Carl
Gustav Jung. From the start, Lüthi insists that the tale's psychological allegiances owe more to the nationality and personality of
the teller than to an archetypal generalization, historical or subliminal. National style is of the highest importance. English and
American versions of "Jack and the Beanstalk," to which we may
turn for a moment in order to illuminate Lüthi's point, set
mother and son in initial conflict with one another—she beats
him because of his foolish bargain—exchanging a cow for a
worthless (but magic) bean. Her substitute in Giant Land, the
ogre's wife, helps Jack win his vindication and the ogre's three

magic objects. But both sides of the Atlantic show their special style. The American's "Fee Faw Fum" rhyme has the giant say "I'll grind his bones/To eat with my pones," and the English bag of gold, hen who lays golden eggs, and singing harp becomes a rifle, a skinnin' knife, and a coverlet with bells. What would a Kentucky hillbilly be without his gun?

Beside the personal style and the national style and the Jungian universal there is a European style; some, indeed, have suggested that the fairy tale is a purely European, or at least an Indo-European, phenomenon. "The Little Earth-Cow" reflects both man and the cosmos: "life and death, good and evil, temptation and intrigue, weakness and innocence, despair, guidance, and assistance," home and the family, nature without and within. From the domestic scene, we move to the mysterious Erce of the Old English charm, to the polarities of "the princess and the swineherd; of the wedding feast and death by execution; and of a little earth-cow that provides silk and velvet and lives in a little house." Magic, like modern science, triumphs over nature. But the power brings taboo. Nature is both good and evil—dragon and earthcow, harmful and helpful animal, kind Gretel and her unkind step-relatives. In overcoming nature, we must also overcome the dark forces within ourselves. We must burn our skin to disenchant ourselves, like the monster bridegrooms of the fairy tale. Has modern man, despite his flirtation with the deeper psyche, forgotten the last of these conflicts? Lüthi achieves meaning for the tale with genuine symbolism, but without "displacement," "cathexis," "archetype," "libido," "mythologem," or any other compromising term. The approach is novel but attractive.

In discussing "The Seven Sleepers," Lüthi was concerned with a saint's legend rather than a local legend. With "The Living Doll," he turns to the unvarnished local story, which is local and individual—and which, like the American ghost story, a widespread form of local legend on our shores, dips into the wellsprings of personal fear. Our phantom housewives, vanishing hitchhikers, and spooks of the mine and the valley parallel the ghosts of the sophisticated Henry James, with his *Turn of the Screw* and "Jolly Corner." A Swissman is a proper man to talk of

local legends. One of the best collections in the world is three
volumes from one small canton, Josef Müller's *Sagn aus Uri*.
From it, Lüthi takes the story of the baptized Tunsch doll, which
comes alive and subjects its creator to many horrors. The local
legend has a personal immediacy, a cruelty, and a directness
glossed over in the fairy tale. The bloody flaying of the cowherd
contrasts with Rumpelstiltskin's hygienic dissection; "The Maiden
without Hands," so close to Chaucer's "Merchant's Tale," is beautiful despite her disability; Lüthi's contrasting Greek tale of "Mr.
Simigdáli" has a hero elsewhere known as "the sugar man," who
is, in one of his apotheoses, the handsome Cupid of Apuleius.
God rules the fairy tale; uncanny forces the Tunsch legend. Even
in "Mr. Simigdáli," there is an anti-heroine as well as a heroine,
and the creation of the sugar man, or man of groats, is a narcissistic act; evil is displaced but not forgotten. The cowherd's
Tunsch doll is likewise narcissistic, but there, Dr. Frankenstein is
overcome by his monster, whereas in the fairy tale, the creation
leads out of one's self into love. Sublimation (Lüthi uses the word
unblushingly) comprehends the erotic and the religious, the
natural and the human, the cosmos; from chaos we come to inte-
gration and order. In this sense, the fairy tale is clearly
medieval and hierarchical, more available to us today as such
than the extant social system of the Middle Ages. Stability, so
essential a matter in the definition of the folk tale and in the
determination of a folk-tale type, becomes an element as well in
its appeal, its use, its symbolism, and its comprehension.

Folklorists make other genre distinctions besides local legend,
saint's legend, and fairy tale. Current everywhere is the animal
story, an ancient form, found among primitive tale tellers. In
Indian America, Polynesia, and Africa, the genres of native tellers
are essentially undifferentiated, but the animal element is ubiq-
uitous. It is also present in Europe, but here it is highly differentiated, into the simple just-so story, the allegorized bestiary, the
moralized fable, and the satirical beast epic of Reynard the Fox.
In tribal cultures, the animal tale comprises the mythical, the
fabulous, and the wonderful alike. Lüthi realizes, as earlier students had done before him, that much we call "wonderful" or

"fairylike" or "enchanted" is simple reality to the primitive mind. Luckily, however, he stops short of the nineteenth-century reconstructive techniques of Gomme, Hartland, and Frazer, which made any slight departure from accepted modern scientific truth a survival of pagan practice. To us, shape-shifting is a narrative device, and remains so even though the primitive mind accepts it as a power owned by the shaman and his god. Lüthi's social interpretation of these phenomena is not as positivistic and innocent as that of Gomme; its symbolism makes it broader. From American Indians comes the small flea, hitchhiking in his race with the gigantic ostrich; it is David against Goliath once more, a mighty mite with whom both primitive and modern minds can identify. In South America, nature is more savage: the victorious horsefly calls in his friends and they feast on the loser's corpse. As Aldous Huxley once said. "Wordsworth's nature would not have been so serene if he had lived in the tropics." The long African tale of Mrile is a tragic story, once more about a living doll, with a shadowy Nemesis but with no commanding Zeus. But like other holistic art, it has humor as well, and reason does not give wholly way to the dark mother or the imbedded ritual.

With Chapter 8 and Rapunzel, we come back to the familiar ground of the Grimms. Here, we see Wilhelm turning the fairy of the original tale recorded by Jacob into a witch, a clarification which demonstrates the tale's kinship to the stregas and lamias of Mediterranean Europe. The comparative method provides meaning as well as history, for Maltese versions reflect the rites of passage by which a girl can mature. "Every process of development and maturation demands great bravery; to let go, to take leave, requires courage." Children, to whom we are inclined to be overprotective, show ample courage; to deprive them of tales of violence is to transfer to them our own fears and thus to keep them from facing up to the facts of life. The ancient witch not only represents the wicked establishment, she is also the disordered terror of the adult world. Lüthi shows that Rapunzel is actually a reconstruction by the Grimms of a seventeenth-century art tale; they worked much as Scott did in creating the ballad "Kinmont Willie" or in injecting moving poetry into "The Wife of Usher's

Well." Lüthi has the talent to make historical scholarship a vivid matter for the reader, much as Richard Altick did for literary scholarship in *The Scholar Adventures*.

Another folk genre is the *novella*, a complex tale without the element of wonder. The riddle princess and the king and the abbot provide conflicts of intelligence: this time, the weak against the strong, the youngest against the eldest. Sometimes our realistically directed children grow out of fairy tales too early for their sentimental parents; but they pursue us with riddles wherever we seek to escape them. I have seen the American ballad fragment of Child 46, "I Gave My Love a Cherry," hold children spellbound; and no wonder, for it holds the riddle of life. Like the symbolism of the fairy tale, the riddling question shoots at an *O altitudo*: "How deep is the ocean? How high is the sky?" Christ's parables were often paradoxes in the same tradition; he reduced the riddling Sadducees with the perfect answer: "In the resurrection they neither marry, nor are given in marriage, but are as the angels of God in heaven." The creative wit of the poet renews itself through the creative wit of the folk riddle, the clever peasant girl in action.

Realizing that many of his tales have shown the feminine nature of many of the Grimms' informants, Lüthi now concerns himself with the hero. The masculine must not be forgotten. Man, indeed, stands at the center of the fairy tale, just as gods and saints inhabited the two kinds of legend, and the animal the primitive tale. Fantastic and wondrous as fairy tales seem, they are closer to humanity than we think or perhaps care to admit. Lutz Röhrich's remarkable study of *Fairy Tale and Reality*, which badly needs translation into English, lies behind the present chapter. The basic domestic conflicts, deeply rooted in the psyche, the elements of social mobility, are real no matter what covert wishes accompany them; wishes themselves make man live and move. Pessimism cannot destroy the truth that some men are better within than appearance makes them, or that some men can move beyond their childhood status no matter how hard the challenge from outmoded social structures and sibling hang-ups. Movement has never been absent from any society: oligarchic,

monarchic, democratic, socialistic. Though Kentucky hillbillies
are laughed at for their insertion of kings into their ballads and
tales, for them the kings are realities. A success story need not be
wholly material; it may be a matter of personal maturing and of
discovery, both by others of the child and by the child of himself.
The local legend, tight-knit and constricted, may regress, but the
fairy tale aspires. "The fairy tale is a poetic vision of man and his
relationship to the world—a vision that for centuries inspired the
fairy tale's hearers with strength and confidence because they
sensed the fundamental truth of this vision." Isolating techniques
of the fairy tale, sharp and two dimensional, offer a basis for
confidence which, to cold reason, appears to be oversimplification.
But if we take fairy tales away from children and give them in-
fantile soap operas instead, children will instinctively find
Tolkien's *Lord of the Rings,* with its simple, unblushing melo-
drama. Let us pray that the simplicity is a decent one. Our com-
plexities do not keep us out of Davos or out of Dachau. A poet of
the absurd, like Kafka, inserts simplicities into his anti-fairy tales;
there is nothing complex about his *Amerika,* a European's view
of the Wild West, and the meaning of that labyrinthine novel,
The Trial, is as plain as the nose on your face. It should not be
forgotten that the fairy tale is art, and that simplicity in the midst
of an almost intolerable diversity is one of the gains of art. Out of
the complex multifoliate rose of Dante comes the great simplicity,
"in His will is our peace."

The eighteenth and nineteenth centuries chose a view of
history which assumed that the world was to be slowly purged of a
cluttering sense of the miraculous. Lessing dramatically dethroned
wonder in *Nathan the Wise,* and the romantics after him con-
tinuously sought to replace the God his generation took away
from them. As Hillis Miller has recently shown us, Keats and
Arnold and even Hopkins were engaged in a rhythm of loss and
search. By calling the fairy tale unrealistic, the Romantic movement preserved it as a very necessary relic. Everyone knows how
realists like Hauptmann, Ibsen, Joyce, and even Dreiser had
to return to the miraculous, the symbolic, the fairylike. Perhaps if
we all sought more fervently the sense of the miraculous in litera-

ture, and ceased to expect it so naïvely in society, we might further our growth as individuals and hence as social beings. Meanwhile, the oral tale and its literary versions remain alive, and Lüthi has shown us how to gain both knowledge and power from them.

In this slender book, Max Lüthi has gathered for us some of the rich harvest of continental study of the folk tale, from his predecessors and contemporaries and from his own ripely speculative mind. His example will be welcomed in America, where we badly need wonder once again in these days of cynicism, which does not become us.

FRANCIS LEE UTLEY

Columbus, Ohio

CHAPTER 1

SLEEPING BEAUTY

The Meaning and Form
of Fairy Tales

Our attitude toward fairy tales (*Märchen*) is ambivalent. "Don't tell me any fairy tales," we say, in the derogatory sense. Here, the term is only a politer expression for cleverly contrived lies. On the other hand, when we admire something especially beautiful, the word *märchenhaft* (i.e., like a fairy tale) almost spontaneously comes to mind. Here, it does not mean unreal in the sense of untrue, but in the sense of unearthy or divine. Thus, even in everyday usage, our language suggests both rejection of, and fascination by, the fairy tale.

For centuries, educated people have looked down on popular fairy tales as stories properly belonging in the nursery and the servants' quarters; yet great writers have repeatedly drawn inspiration from them. Great literature of all ages has borrowed from fairy-tale motifs and often exhibited an imaginativeness not unlike that of the fairy tale. In the life of the individual, there are periods when one is fascinated by fairy tales and periods of indifference. After the actual fairy-tale age (between five and ten), there follows a realistic stage during which one is ill-dis-

posed toward fairy tales. Some people persist in this attitude all
their lives. But in others, understanding and love for these once-
coveted stories returns later in life, not only because now as
mothers or grandfathers they themselves are called upon to tell
fairy tales, but just as much because they again feel moved by
their peculiar charm.

When something has the ability both to attract and repel one
so forcefully, one may assume that it deals with fundamentals.
One is challenged to take sides, explicitly or implicitly. The role
fairy tales play in the lives of children, and the role they played
in the lives of adults in the millennia prior to the coming of the
printed word, strengthens us in the belief that we are dealing
with a peculiar form of literature, one which concerns man directly.

When we speak of fairy tales today, we cannot help thinking of the collection by the Grimm brothers—and this applies not
only to the region where German is spoken. *Grimm's Fairy Tales*,
which first appeared in 1812 and 1815, is in many countries the
most popular, the most oft-reprinted German book. Even among
primitive folk they show their great effect: the Grimm tales mis-
sionaries have told to natives in some cases have the power to
supplant indigenous tales. In the following passage from "Sleeping Beauty," one of the best-known tales in the Grimm collection,
certain basic features of the fairy tale can be discovered. The
introductory section reads as follows:

> Once upon a time there was a king and a queen and every day
> they said, "O, if we only had a child!" But they never had one. Now
> it happened one day while the queen was sitting in her bath that a
> frog came out of the water, crept ashore and said to the queen,
> "Your wish will be fulfilled; before a year goes by you will give
> birth to a daughter." This happened just as the frog had said it
> would and the queen gave birth to a girl so beautiful that the king
> was beside himself with joy and ordered a great feast. He invited
> not only his relatives, friends and acquaintances, but also the Wise
> Women, so that they would be well-disposed and feel kindly
> toward the child. There were in his realm thirteen of them, but
> because he had only twelve golden plates for them to eat from, one

of them had to stay at home. The feast was celebrated with great splendor, and when it was over the Wise Women presented the child with their magic gifts. One gave virtue, the next beauty, the third wealth, and thus everything desirable that there is in the world. Just as the eleventh had announced her gift the thirteenth suddenly walked in. She wanted her revenge because she had not been invited, and without a greeting or even a glance at anyone she cried in a loud voice, "The princess shall in her fifteenth year be pricked by a spindle and fall down dead." And without saying another word she turned around and left the hall. Everyone was dismayed. Then the twelfth Wise Woman who still had her wish came forward, and because she could not break the spell but only modify it, she said, "But it will not be death. The princess will fall into a deep sleep that will last for one hundred years."

Everyone knows how the tale goes on from here. The king's decree "that all spindles in the entire kingdom be burned" cannot save the child. When she is fifteen years old, she pricks herself with a spindle (which arouses her interest for the very reason that she has never seen one before), and at once falls asleep under the magic spell, together with the king, the queen, and the whole royal household. All around the palace there grows a dense hedge of thorns. The princes who try to force their way through are caught and held in the thorns, where they suffer greatly. After exactly 100 years, another prince ventures forth. Now, instead of thorns, there are only big, beautiful flowers which separate by themselves, permitting him to pass through unharmed, and then they close again behind him. The prince's kiss brings the sleeping princess back to life again, the whole household awakens with her, and a splendid wedding is celebrated.

The Grimm brothers themselves wondered about the meaning of this fairy tale, which appears in a similar form among other peoples. What is its core, its essence? What does it stand for? Jacob and Wilhelm Grimm saw in fairy tales remnants of ancient myths, playful descendants of an ancient intuitive vision of life and the world. Sleeping Beauty, wondrously endowed and mysteriously threatened, suffers death or a sleep similar to death. But she is awakened again and begins to flourish—and with her, the

strongly evident even in this brief introduction to "Sleeping Beauty."

We love the fairy tale not only for its wisdom, but the manner in which it is told; its external appearance, which varies from people to people and from narrator to narrator, also delights us. The Grimm brothers' genius for storytelling is likewise evident in the very first part of the fairy tale. The entire first section is based on the motif of prophecy. Once stated, the theme is varied and intensified. The birth of the little girl is heralded by a frog and the Wise Women bestow on her virtue, beauty, wealth, and other miraculous gifts, that is to say, they proclaim all this. But the thirteenth fairy—and here one anxiously holds his breath —prophesies that the princess will die in her fifteenth year. Following this climax—which is strongly underlined by the sudden bursting upon the scene of the fairy who had been neglected, by her short, loud words and her silent departure—the tension in the story gradually subsides. A final variation on the prophecy motif, the conversion of the death pronouncement into the proclamation of the 100-year sleep, relieves the inner tension, but at once gives rise to the question of how and whether the proclamation will come true and what will happen during and after the enchanted sleep. A truly dramatic exposition!

A comparison of the Grimm brothers' original notations with the final version of "Sleeping Beauty" shows what their poetic imagination and genius for language has added. No one familiar with the tale can forget the humorous description of the palace as it sinks into sleep and reawakens. The passage reads:

> This sleep spread throughout the palace. The king and queen, who had returned home and had just entered the hall, began to fall asleep along with their entire royal household. The horses, too, fell asleep in their stables, as did the dogs in the courtyard, the pigeons on the roof, and the flies on the wall. Even the fire flickering in the hearth subsided and went to sleep, and the roast stopped sizzling. The cook, who was about to pull the kitchen-boy's hair for forgetting something, let him go and slept. The wind, too, subsided, and not a leaf stirred any more in the trees around the palace.

What, now, was in Jacob Grimm's notes when he first recorded this fairy tale, which previously had been transmitted by word of mouth? Only this: "Since at this moment the king and his royal household also returned, everybody and everything in the palace—right down to the flies on the wall—began to sleep." The little parenthetical remark "right down to the flies on the wall" inspired the Grimm brothers to draw this picture with its leisurely descriptions and wealth of characters. They give even freer play to their imagination in the concluding section. The original notes ended in this way: "Now as he entered the palace he kissed the sleeping princess, everyone awakened, and the two were married and lived happily ever after." In the Grimm brothers' collection, this single sentence becomes the following:

> In the courtyard of the castle he saw the horses and the spotted hunting dogs lying asleep, and on the roof the pigeons sat with their little heads tucked under their wings. And when he entered the house the flies were asleep on the wall, the cook in the kitchen still had his hand stretched out as if he were about to grab the boy, and the maid sat before the black chicken which was to be plucked. He continued on, and in the hall he saw the entire royal household lying asleep—and, up by the throne, the king and queen. And he went still further, but everything was so quiet that one could hear himself breathing, and finally he came to the tower and opened the door to the little room where Sleeping Beauty lay asleep. She was so beautiful that he could not turn his eyes away from her, and he stooped down and gave her a kiss. When his lips touched her she opened her eyes, awakened, and looked at him very kindly. Then they walked down together, and the king and queen and the entire royal household awakened and looked at each other in great astonishment. And the horses in the courtyard stood up and shook themselves, the hunting dogs leapt up, wagging their tails, and the pigeons on the roof took their little heads out from under their wings, looked about and flew off to the fields. The flies on the wall continued crawling, the fire in the kitchen flared up and cooked the meal, the roast began to sizzle again, the cook gave the boy such a slap that he howled, and the maid finished plucking the chicken. Then the marriage of the prince and Sleeping Beauty was celebrated with great pomp, and they lived happily to their life's end.

In the final sentence the Grimm brothers return to the actual fairy-tale style, which, in a few well-chosen words, merely suggests the sequence of events, and which has a preference for action rather than lengthy descriptions. We are delighted that here the editors paint a leisurely picture of the two central events: when the palace falls asleep and when it reawakens. In other places they avoid detailed descriptions. They do not go into any details of the wedding celebration, and they summarize the birthday celebration at the beginning in a manner characteristic of the fairy tale, in a single sentence: "The celebration was observed with great pomp." On the other hand, when they allow themselves the pleasure of describing in its grotesque aspect how life comes to a halt and then suddenly begins to dance again—it is as if the figures on a music box had stopped and now, after the apparatus has been rewound, automatically begin to turn again— there is an irony at work which appeals to children as well as to adults. The love scene is thereby deprived of all sentimentality; it develops and unfolds unperceived and pure in the protection of the comical elements which surround it.

It must now be clear that the Grimm brothers did not retell the fairy tales exactly as they heard them. On the contrary, they carefully edited them, simplifying or embellishing them according to their poetic inclinations and pedagogical intentions. Not infrequently, they combined several variants of one and the same fairy tale: they chose from each tale what seemed to them the best. Naturally, they were not completely independent of the spirit and the taste of their times, the era of romanticism and the *Biedermeier* culture with its painful loss of idealism and acceptance of reality. The romantic charm of forest and flowers and playful romantic irony combine with the warmth and intimacy basic to the outlook on life in the *Biedermeier*. But if *Grimm's Fairy Tales* have lived on far past their era and have won the hearts of the world, if they also appeal to us today, and if not only the story, but the manner in which it is told delights us—all this shows once again that both styles are not merely historical: the era of romanticism and the era of the *Biedermeier* merely revealed in a particularly pure and powerful form feelings that are possible at all times and in every person.

The classical fairy-tale collections of other peoples date from other eras. The most famous Italian fairy-tale book is the *Pentamerone,* fifty stories which the Neapolitan writer Giambattista Basile compiled at the beginning of the seventeenth century, many of them popular tales previously kept alive by oral tradition. While they are written in the dialect of Naples, Basile also did not retell the fairy tales exactly as he heard them; he fashioned them to his taste. It was the taste of the baroque era. Since our own century has developed a new understanding for baroque style, we are now especially receptive to Basile's charming and humorous tales. The fifth story on the fifth day bears the title "Sun, Moon and Talia." It is similar to our "Sleeping Beauty." The beginning reads as follows:

> Once upon a time a nobleman had a daughter, and when she was born he had all the wise men and soothsayers in the kingdom come together for the purpose of prophesying her fate. Now after much deliberation they asserted she was in great peril because of a thread of flax. For this reason, and to guard against any mishaps, her father sent out a strict order that neither flax nor hemp nor anything like them should ever be brought to his palace. But one day when Talia had grown older and was standing at a window, she saw an old woman who was spinning as she walked by. Since the girl had never before seen either distaff or spindle and was intrigued by how they turned back and forth, she was overcome by such great curiosity that she had the old woman sent up and, taking the distaff in hand, began to spin the thread. But while doing this she unfortunately was pricked under a fingernail by a hemp fiber and at once fell down dead. As soon as the old woman saw this, she fled down the stairs; but the poor father, informed of the mishap, paid for this cup of sorrow with barrels of tears. Then he had his dead daughter set on a velvet throne under a canopy of brocade in the summer palace where he was then staying, and at once closed all the doors and forsook this place which had been the source of such calamity, so that he might banish the memory of these events for ever and ever.

Thus, Basile makes no mention of either the prophetic frog or the wishes of the fairies, an indication of how unrelated such figures are to the core of the tale. But here, too, the motif of prophecy and with it the threat of an unavoidable fate is clearly expressed. As in the Grimm tale—and even more clearly here—it is just the attempts to avoid fate which provoke the calamity: only because the girl is unaccustomed to the sight of spindle and hemp is she so anxious to take them in hand. One instinctively thinks of the use of prophesy in the ancient Oedipus myth. It is fascinating to see how the baroque style of the seventeenth century is manifested in Basile's narrative: the baroque love for pomp sets the dead Talia on a velvet throne under a canopy of brocade; the baroque sense of humor has the father cry barrels full of tears; the manneristic-baroque fondness for abrupt changes has him forget his beloved daughter immediately thereafter "for ever and ever." The following section from the Italian fairy tale introduces a motif we do not find in Grimm:

> But it happened one day when the king was out hunting that a falcon slipped from his hand and flew in through a window of that castle. Since the bird did not come when they called it, the king, believing the castle to be occupied, ordered his men to knock on the door. But after they had knocked a long time in vain the king sent for a vintager's ladder, so he might enter, too, and see how it looked inside. After he had wandered all through it he was completely beside himself with astonishment at finding not a living soul inside. But finally he came to the room where the enchanted princess lay, and he called her, believing her to be asleep. But since she did not awaken no matter how much he shouted at her and shook her, and since he was enraptured by her beauty, he took her away in his arms to a place where he lay down with her and there picked the fruits of love. Hereupon, leaving her lying on the bed, he returned to his kingdom, where he did not think of this event again for a long time.
>
> But after nine months had passed Talia gave birth to twins, a boy and a girl who were like two precious jewels and were well cared for in every way by two fairies who appeared in the palace and put them to suck on their mother's breasts. Now when the twins wanted to suck again and could not find the nipples, they

> took hold of a finger and sucked on it until they pulled out the fiber. Hereupon Talia seemed to awaken as if from a deep sleep, gave suck to the little angels she found next to her and grew to love them with all her heart. But she had absolutely no idea what had happened to her, since she saw that she was completely alone in the palace with the two sucklings and was brought food and drink by invisible hands.

Jacob Grimm considered it especially delightful that the child sucks the flax fiber out of the sleeping mother's finger. And, indeed, this type of awakening, which combines, in baroque fashion, the natural and the fantastic, has its own charm. The kiss which redeems Sleeping Beauty in the Grimm version has no obvious connection with the cause of the enchantment, the prick of the spindle. But Basile's variant has a sort of artistic economy: the flax fiber which puts Talia to sleep plays a role again in her awakening. And it is especially delightful and significant that the children unintentionally and unknowingly bring about the actual redemption of Sleeping Beauty.

We also find a variant of Sleeping Beauty in the oldest French fairy-tale book, the *Contes de ma mère l'Oye* of Charles Perrault. Perrault was an architect of the late seventeenth century and a member of the French Academy during the high point of French classicism. In 1697 he published eight fairy tales which, in contrast with the many freely embellished tales of fairies and pixies in fashion at the time, give clear evidence of their origin among the common people. *La belle au bois dormant* ("The Sleeping Beauty in the Forest") stands at the head of the collection. The passage of the awakening of the princess may serve as a sample of Perrault's style:

> The prince, trembling and full of wonder, approached the sleeping woman and fell on his knees before her. Because the end of the spell had now come, the princess awakened and looked at him with fonder eyes than is really proper at first meeting and said to him: "Is it you, my prince? You have been a long time in coming." The prince was delighted by these words, and even more by the way she said them. He did not know how he might show his

joy and declare his affection for her. He asserted that he loved her
more than himself. His speech was a little incoherent, but this just
made it all the more pleasing—little eloquence, much love. His
embarrassment was greater than hers, and that is not surprising:
she, after all, had had time to think about what she would say to
him.

Later, the story goes on:

> The prince, trembling and full of wonder, approached the
> splendid attire. But he was careful not to tell her that she was
> dressed like his grandmother with her stiff collar—she was no less
> beautiful because of it. They entered a hall of mirrors and dined
> there, attended by the princess's manservants. The violins and
> oboes played old compositions—excellent pieces, though they had
> been seldom played for nearly 100 years. After the supper no time
> was lost: the priest married them in the chapel and the maid of
> honor drew the curtain. They had little sleep: the princess did not
> need it just then and the prince left her early in the morning to
> return to town, where his father must have been worrying about
> him.

Here again we find a style differing from that of the Grimm
brothers; it is the irony of the seventeenth-century courtly *salon*,
and it is directed at the pair of lovers themselves, not just at their
surroundings. But here, too, the irony adds spice to the tale without impairing its basic structure. Perrault cannot forgo the pleasure of making the passage of the 100 years clearly felt by his
repeated observations. In doing this, he violates the style of the
popular fairy tale, with its characteristic disregard for the passage
of time, as the Grimm brothers do when they refrain from calling
Sleeping Beauty's dress old-fashioned. But Perrault's irony is only
on the surface of his tale; its indifference to the decay which time
always brings about in the world of men is stressed all the more
by his smiling allusions. The second part of his fairy tale resem-
bles Basile's. Perrault's heroine also gives birth to two children,
but their names are not *Sole e Luna* (Sun and Man), as in
Basile's tale, but *Aurore et Jour* (Dawn and Day). Basile and

Perrault both relate how these children and the heroine herself have to suffer persecution at the hands of an evil queen, how they are to be killed and how they are saved through the compassion of the hired assassin. Is this last part of the fairy tale merely an accidental appendage, taken arbitrarily from another fairy tale in order to lengthen the tale? The theme of the death prophesy and the fortunate deliverance is once again called to mind. Even if this last section should be of external origin, it fits in well as a variation on the basic theme.

The comparison of the different variants shows that we must be cautious about our interpretation of details. The names sun and moon, dawn and day, as they are found in Basile and Perrault, strengthened the Grimm brothers in their belief that a natural process is reflected in the Sleeping Beauty tale. In this respect, we will not raise any objection. But when they claim to see a symbol for dawn in the hedge of roses and, likewise, in the wall of flames surrounding the sleeping Nordic Brynhild, we arrive at a point where interpretations become problematical. Narrow and rigid interpretations cannot be ascribed to a dynamic story. Can we see, in the twelve fairies, the twelve months which bestow their manifold gifts on the earth and on nature? The thirteenth fairy who has been provoked to anger would then be—yes, such suggestions have been made in all seriousness—the personification of the unthroned, neglected thirteenth month; and the whole thing would portray the transition from the lunar year, with its thirteen months, to the solar year, with its twelve. The 100 years, it is explained, is nothing more than a poetic overstatement for the 100 days of winter, when the earth lies imprisoned in sleep. With such sophistical allegorizing the natural-mythological interpretation is carried to absurdity. We need look no further than Perrault's variant, where the entire theory is unacceptable, for Perrault speaks not of twelve good fairies, but of seven. One must guard against the desire to interpret every single feature, every thorn and every fly. Some of these details are mere ornamentation added by whomever told the story last. Seven and twelve are popular fairy-tale numbers, and one should not presume each time that a mystery lies behind them. Yet the

three variants discussed—joined by a large number of versions
recorded at different times and among various peoples—lead us
to believe that, in the over-all course of events, a significant, constantly recurring process is at work: danger and redemption,
paralysis and rejuvenation, death and resurrection. The individual compilers cast the fairy tale in the garb of their time, and
the tension between the inner form and the outer garb of the
fairy tale can be particularly charming for those with fastidious
tastes. In any event, we would not care to do without the elegance
and incisiveness of Perrault, the sensitivity and refinement of the
Grimm brothers, the power and vitality of Basile—or the humor
which characterizes all three tales. Basile's often indelicate jokes
are not intended for children; but the two other tales have the
power to charm and exhilarate both children and adults.

CHAPTER 2

THE SEVEN SLEEPERS

Saint's Legend
Local Legend
Fairy Tale

In former times, when there were no radios and few books, when stories were told among a group gathered for the evening, no special name was given to them. They were simply tales, stories, *contes, Geschichten.* Every language and every dialect has such an over-all term. In the Hasli Valley in the canton of Bern (Switzerland), they were *Zelleni,* in Lorraine, *Gschichte* or *Rätsle,* in northern Germany, *Vertelsel* or *Löögschen* (that is, lies). The precise terms *Märchen* (fairy tale), *Sage* (local legend), *Legende* (Saint's legend), *Schwank* (farce) have gained favor only through the scholar. The common folk who told the tales originally used the terms, if at all, only in their general meaning: *Märchen* (in medieval German *maerlin*) means, after all, nothing but a little tale, a brief story; and *Sage* (*cf.* English "say") means what is said or told. The original teller of the local legend believed his tale and by no means wanted to characterize it as legendary in our sense. And yet, the distinctions made by scholarly analysis have their justification. The rich store of tales which were once handed down only by oral tradition can really be separated into a relatively small number of types which have coexisted for some time. The genres realistic story, fairy tale, saint's legend, and local legend have taken shape in the course of millennia and have been retained in quite pure form for many epochs. Each of these genres seems to serve an elementary human need. They may deal with similar themes, but they do it in a different way. At the end of their *Fairy Tales*, beginning with the second edition, the Grimm brothers added a number of tales which they called "children's legends." One of them tells of the twelve apostles.

The Twelve Apostles

Three hundred years before the birth of our Lord there lived a mother who had twelve sons. But she was so pitifully poor that she didn't know how she could keep them alive any longer. Every day she prayed to God and pleaded with Him to allow all her sons to be with the promised Savior on earth. Now as her distress became greater, she sent one after the other out into the world to seek their own livelihood. The oldest, named Peter, went forth and had gone quite far—an entire day's journey—when he came to a great forest. He sought a way out, but could not find one and wandered deeper and deeper into the forest. He was so hungry that he could barely stand, and finally became so weak that he had to lie down. He believed himself to be on the verge of death when suddenly there stood before him a small boy who gave forth a great light and was as handsome and kind as an angel. The child clapped its little hands together, so that Peter raised his eyes and looked at the child. Then the child said, "Why do you sit there so sadly?" "Alas," Peter answered, "I wander about in the world and seek my bread, so that I may someday see the dear, promised Savior: that is my greatest wish." The child said, "Come with me, and your wish shall be ful-filled." The child took the poor man by the hand and guided him around great blocks of stone into a large cave. There everything sparkled with gold, silver and crystal, and in the middle stood twelve cradles side by side. Then the little angel spoke: "Lie down in the first one and sleep a little, and I will rock you." This Peter did, and the little angel sang to him and rocked him until he had fallen asleep. Now while he was sleeping, the second brother came, also led there by his guardian angel, and was rocked to sleep just like the first brother. And the other brothers came, too, one after the other, until all twelve lay there sleeping in the golden cradles. Now they slept for three hundred years, until the night in which the Savior of the World was born. And then they awakened and were with him on the earth and were called the twelve apostles.

The Latin word *legenda* means "that which is to be read." This very name reveals to us something of the nature of the saint's legend. It is a story which one can *read*; it has not, like the fairy tale, been entrusted to those who transmit by word of mouth —the workers and servants—but has been written down, namely by clerics. The most famous medieval collection of saints' legends is the *Legenda Aurea* (the Golden Legend Book) of Jacobus a Voragine, written between 1245 and 1273. Its editor, Jacopo of Varazze, became archbishop of Genoa a few years later. Thus, the saints' legends circulating among the common folk were not disregarded or dispised like the fairy tale: the church watched over them and cared for them. And this now suggests a second thing: the saint's legend is not only a story one *can* read, it is also a story one *should* read. It is believed to have the power to edify the faithful and strengthen them in their belief. It tells about the saints, from unknown local saints or their relics all the way up to Christ and Mary. Its core is the miracle: it bears witness to the contact of holy persons with God and the supernatural. The original miracle is the resurrection, which is reflected in many forms in saints' legends. The decapitated martyr comes back to life by a miracle, the sick man is cured by a miracle. Grimm's children's legend of the twelve apostles is in this respect completely like the saint's legend in character—its theme is a miraculous resurrection. But the style is entirely that of the *Fairy Tales*. Wilhelm Grimm, who revised the *Fairy Tales* almost single-handedly from the second edition on, avoids subordinate clauses: "It was three hundred years before the birth of our Lord. There lived a mother. She had twelve sons." From time to time, he slips in short direct quotations. As in the fairy tale, everything sparkles with gold, silver, and crystal; and the warm-hearted, sentimental tone

of the teller—something we are accustomed to in Wilhelm
Grimm—permeates the entire tale: "The boy was as handsome
and kind as an angel." The 300 years pass without any visible
effect on the sleeping brothers, just as they did for Sleeping
Beauty. The event is removed to a great distance in time—300
years before Christ's birth—and the entire tale has something delightfully playful about it. One can hardly speak here of a genuine religious belief, unless it is a childlike faith. The story right-
fully bears the name "children's legend." We can see how the real
saint's legend treats a similar theme. The story "The Seven
Sleepers" appears in Jacobus a Voragine's *Legenda Aurea*. It tells
how the Roman emperor Decius put to death all the inhabitants
of Ephesus who would not offer sacrifices to the heathen gods.
Seven fine Christian youths hid in a cave, and as they sat there
together, talking and weeping, the Lord suddenly put them to
sleep and saved them from the hands of their pursuers.

Three hundred and seventy-two years passed, Decius and all
his family had long since died, and it was the thirtieth year of the
reign of Theodosius. It so happened now that the heresy spread
which says that there is no resurrection of the dead. Theodosius,
who was a devoutly Christian emperor, was deeply saddened at
seeing the faith threatened by such blasphemy, and put on a hair
shirt and kneeled in the innermost room of his palace and cried
day and night. Now the merciful Lord saw his sorrow and wanted
to console those who were saddened and strengthen the hope of
resurrection from the dead. He therefore opened up His great store
of love and awakened the seven martyrs. They greeted one another
and thought only that they had slept overnight. Remembering
their former grief they asked Malchus, who had been the last to
bring them food, what Decius had decided to do about them. And
Malchus answered just as he had the evening before: "We will be
taken prisoner and forced to make sacrifices to the idols. That is
the emperor's decree." Maximianus answered: "The Lord knows
we shall never sacrifice to the idols." And he comforted his com-
panions and asked Malchus to go to town to buy some bread, and
told him to bring more bread than the day before. He also was to
inform them about what else the emperor had decreed. Thus,
Malchus took five small coins and left the cave. Full of fear he

approached the gate to the city, on which he was greatly astonished to see the sign of the cross. He continued walking to the other city gate, where he also perceived a cross. This astonished him beyond all measure. And when he saw that the cross was on all the gates to the city, and the city itself was completely changed, he crossed himself—for he believed he was dreaming. Now he returned to the first gate and, summoning up all his courage, covered his face and entered the city.

No one knows him, and he is brought before the bishop and the proconsul. An old letter is found recounting the events of many years ago, and now the bishop sees that God wanted to perform a miracle with this youth. He summons the people together, leads them to the entrance to the cave of the seven resurrected men, and has the letter read to the public.

When they had heard it they were all greatly astonished and looked into the cave and saw the saints sitting there with rosy faces. Then they all cast themselves down at the brothers' feet and praised God. But the bishop and the pronconsul immediately sent word to the emperor Theodosius in Constantinople and bade him to come at once and see the miracle which God had just performed. And thus the emperor arose from his sackcloth and ashes in which he had been mourning, praised the Lord and started out on his way to Ephesus. The people all went forth to meet him and accompanied him to the cave. When saints saw the emperor, their faces began to glow like the sun. But the emperor entered, cast himself at their feet and praised God. Then he arose, embraced them and exclaimed, "When I see you I feel as if I were witnessing the Lord raising Lazarus." Then Maximianus said to him, "Know that the Lord has resurrected us before the great Day of Resurrection for your sake, so that you will have no doubts and will believe in the resurrection of the dead. For behold, we have truly arisen from the dead, and are alive. And like the child who lives in its mother's womb and suffers no harm we too lay sleeping here, alive but feeling nothing." Everyone watched as the saints spoke these words, bowed their heads to the ground, fell asleep and gave up the ghost according to God's will. Then the emperor arose, and, shedding many tears, threw himself upon them, and kissed them. Then he ordered that golden coffins be made to lay them in. But during the night they appeared to him and told him to leave them just as they had been until now, lying in the earth from which they had arisen, until the Lord brings them back to life for a second time. Thus, the emperor merely had the spot marked by stones adorned with gold leaf. Then he decreed an indulgence for all bishops who believed in the resurrection of the dead. However, it is questionable whether the saints slept 377 years, for they arose in the year of our Lord 448. Decius, however, reigned for only one year and three months, in the year of our Lord 252. It is therefore possible that they slept for only 196 years.

The Grimm brothers' children's legend of the twelve apostles, taken from an oral source in Paderborn, seems to be patterned somewhat after "The Seven Sleepers." The period of 300 years, the bread which the child—as well as the youth—is sent out for, the golden coffins in one tale and the golden cradles in the other, these details have hardly found their way into the two tales independently of one another. However, the emphasis in the version of Jacobus a Voragine is quite different: the story now has the character of an exemplary saint's legend. The presentation is much more realistic. Every situation is motivated with the greatest caution and various events are related to each other. Thus, the baker thinks that the old coins, which Malchus shows to him, are part of an ancient treasure, and since the youth will not confess to having found such a treasure, he is brought before the proconsul. The outward appearance of the city is described in detail, as is the astonishment and fear of the youth upon entering the city. Sleeping Beauty lies in repose for 100 years; in the fairy-tale legend of the twelve apostles, it is 300. But in the saint's legend of the seven sleepers, no such smooth, round numbers appear. The stating of the precise figure of 372 years is intended to inspire our confidence in the reliability of the teller and his tale. The time which has elapsed also has its effect: the city has changed, and the resurrected brothers are in death's clutches despite the miracle which God performs with them. The scene in which, after having spoken, they bow their heads to the ground and expire is unforgettable. The saint's legend exhibits a splendid and striking

blend of realism and stylization. Even the critical concluding remark of Jacobus a Voragine—that the saints most likely did not
sleep 372 or 377 years, but rather 196—impresses us not only as a
scholarly gloss, but seems to be in its proper place at the conclusion of the tale. It re-emphasizes the truth of the tale in contrast
to the fairy-tale ending, which ironically hints at the unreality of
the preceding story: "Whoever believes it pays a thaler." "At the
wedding, too, was I; mead and wine drank I— It flowed over the
moustache mine; but not into this mouth of mine." "Now they
were happy, but we're left sitting here." In addition to the realism of the saint's legend, one can also clearly see the dominant role
of the miracle in the tale of the seven sleepers. The entire tale is
told for the sake of this miracle, to affirm an article of faith, convert
heretics, and strengthen the true believers. The tale is carefully
constructed with this purpose in mind. In the local legend and
also in the fairy tale, one may have the feeling that they have
grown by themselves and are not consciously fashioned; but in
the saint's legend, one feels much more strongly the hand of the
author giving form to his tale. But the real power of the saint's
legend has much deeper roots. The miracle it reports not only
bears witness to an article of faith, but has a fascination of its
own. The power of the miracle is felt in a different way in the
saint's legend, the local legend, and the fairy tale. We compare
the local legend from the canton of Wallis about Prior Evo, who
slept 308 years, and the saint's legend from the Rhineland about
Abbot Erpho.

The Prior Who Slept 308 Years

One day the Prior Evo felt very much like taking a walk after his
meal. He went a little way into the forest but soon felt so tired that
he sat down and listened to a bird which was singing very beautifully in a tree. While listening, he fell asleep. When he awakened
he thought he had slept about a half hour. He started out on his
way back home, but when he caught sight of the monastery it
seemed quite different to him. The gate keeper was a man he had
never seen before and he therefore asked him just who had ap-
pointed him. The gate keeper looked surprised and asked him why

he wanted to know, since he wasn't in any way connected with the monastery. "What!" exclaimed the priest, "I am the prior of this monastery and left here an hour ago to take a little after-dinner nap in the forest!" Upon hearing this, the gate keeper went and got the prior, who called together all the monks and had the stranger brought in. Then the prior asked all those assembled if they knew this man. They all shook their heads. Evo clapped his hand to his forehead in astonishment, and couldn't figure out what all this might mean. The prior remembered having read in the history of the monastery about a priest who had gotten lost many years ago. He now had this chronicle brought to him, and as he leafed through it, found the name Evo in the year 1208—the priest had slept for 308 years in the forest. When Evo heard that, he fell over without making a sound and crumbled into dust and ashes.

Abbot Erpho of Siegburg

Erpho, the first abbot of the monastery of Siegburg and a friend of Bishop Anno of Cologne, was known for his great piety. Every day he selected a passage from the Bible and meditated on it. Thus, one day he read the words of the 90th Psalm: "A thousand years in God's sight are like a yesterday when it is passed." At this, so many doubts arose in his mind that it left him no peace any more. He entered the garden of the monastery, and without watching where he was going, walked further into the neighboring forest. As he was strolling about there under the tall trees, in continuous meditation and doubts, he caught sight of a bird, which looked so strange and wonderful that he thought he had never before seen one like it. It was about as large as a dove, its plumage shone with all the colors of the rainbow, and its song was so beautiful that all the animals in the forest seemed to listen. Erpho, too, listened to the bird's song, and his heart experienced a joy it had never before known. Suddenly the song came to an end, and the abbot perceived that he was already deep in the forest, although he thought he had been listening to the bird's song for only a few minutes. He now hastened to return to the monastery, but as he emerged from the forest his astonishment became greater with every step. Everything was different from what he had known—the monastery, the town, the people he met. When he reached the top of the hill where the monastery was situated, the bells were ringing and the monks were marching about in procession. At their head was a prelate he had never seen before, and no one seemed to know him. He turned to the old gate keeper, who told him that the monastery had been like this for as long as he could remember. The abbot, too, who came along with the priests and friars, looked at him with great respect, but could find no answer to this mystery. Finally, an old monk remembered he had once heard that the Abbot Erpho, 300 years ago, had disappeared from the monastery shortly before vespers and had never returned. They consulted the chronicle in the monastery and found that to be the case. Now they were all certain that it was Abbot Erpho who stood before them. He told them everything that had happened, and they all praised God for performing this miracle. He then proceeded to the church, received Holy Communion, praised God in a loud voice and fell down dead. That occurred on the day after Ascension Day in the year 1367, after the holy man had been gone from the face of the earth since the same day in the year 1067.

It is quite clear that the tale from Upper Wallis about Prior Evo and the one from the Rhineland about Abbot Erpho can not have originated independently of each other, but their tone is clearly different. The Rhenish tale has the tone of a saint's legend; it is didactic. Like the story of the seven sleepers, which seems to serve as its model, it affirms a religious assertion, specifically by means of a miracle. In the tale from Wallis, however, the emphasis has shifted imperceptibly yet decisively: the saint's legend has been transformed into a local legend. The resident of Visperterminen who tells the tale is not concerned with any conflict of dogma. The interest here is directed instead solely at the incomprehensible event. The central point is still the miracle, but it is no longer performed by God for a very special purpose. The milieu and characters are still those of the saint's legend—monastery, prior, gate keeper. But the mysterious event is no longer interpreted. The miracle here does not have the effect of throwing light on concealed relationships and thus assuring the hearer that he lives in a meaningful and divinely ordered world. On the contrary, it confuses him—it is not comprehended. The faces of the seven sleepers shine in the splendor of their trans-

figuration; Abbot Erpho praises God in a loud voice and falls
down dead. But of the Prior Evo from Wallis, it says, "The priest
had slept for 308 years in the forest. When Evo heard that, he fell
over without making a sound and crumbled into dust and ashes."
The event so overwhelms the person concerned that it destroys
him. The saint's legend ends in splendor and glory, the local
legend in dust and ashes. The saint's legend reveals a glorious
religious truth, whereas the local legend reports an uncanny event
which shocks or confuses us. The local legend revolves around the
inexplicable intrusion of a completely different world which cannot be comprehended by the intellect. In the saint's legend, just
the reverse is true: the same unnatural event is a consolation, a
testimony to the existence of a deeper meaning. Both local legend
and saint's legend are, however, relatively realistic in style; they
demonstrate a strong awareness of the passage of time and exhibit
a fascination with the unheard-of event.

What is the situation in the fairy tale? All things in it, persons and events, appear sublimated. It does not have the pon-
derousness of the local legend and the saint's legend. When, in the
local legend from Wallis, the prior collapses the moment he
learns that he has slept without noticing it for 308 years, it is as if
he suddenly becomes aware of the passage of time and in one jolt
catches up wih the present. It is a phenomenon which might have
interested an Henri Bergson. Even in the myths of ancient
Greece, poetic imagination revolved around such things, as is
evident in the tale of Eos and Tithonos. Eos, the goddess of dawn,
pleads for and receives from Zeus immortality for her mortal husband, Tithonos. But she forgot to ask at the same time for eternal
youth, and thus he wastes away at her side, dries out, and shrivels
up until Eos finally turns him into a cricket. In the fairy tale,
however, Sleeping Beauty arises with a smile and is as young and
beautiful and light-hearted as she was 100 years ago. The fairy
tale conquers time by ignoring it. Part of the power which it has
to delight the reader derives from this triumph over time and the
passage of time. Of course it knows of and makes reference to
young and old people, but it does not portray the aging process.
In the local legend, flowering mountain pastures are covered with

ice, magic balls of yarn and cheeses become smaller, grow larger, and finally disappear. Heirlooms link earlier and later generations. In the fairy tale, magic objects are never bequeathed; they are only important when they are used to perform a certain task. On the other hand, when a wicked witch puts out the eyes of the fairy-tale heroine, they can simply be put back again years later, as if they had not decayed. The fairy tale portrays an imperishable world, and this explains its partiality for everything metallic and mineral, for gold and silver, for glass and crystal. The local legend and the saint's legend, however, do exactly the opposite, they make us especially aware of the passage of time and cessation of things. Both of these seem essential to mankind. Just as at certain times we become especially aware of the passage of time (for example, in the final days of the year), certain kinds of tales also remind us of time and transitoriness. But others—specifically the fairy tale and similar genres—remove us from the time continuum and make us feel that there is another way of viewing and experiencing life, that behind all birth and death there is another world, resplendent, imperishable, and incorruptible. Such a world is the theme, material, and contents of the saint's legend; the fairy tale, however, reveals it to us through its *form*.

Our examples show something else: the miracle plays a different role in the fairy tale than in the local legend and saint's legend. A Breton fairy tale with the characteristic title "The Crystal Castle" contains the motif of the person who returns from another world 380 years later. But it stands at the end of a complicated and fantastic tale full of magical events, and thus loses much of its significance. In the local legend and in the saint's legend, the miracle fascinates, moves, frightens, or delights us; in the fairy tale, it is a matter of course. In the local legend and in the saint's legend, the miracle astounds us and is at the heart of the entire tale; in the fairy tale, it is incorporated into a larger sequence of events, it becomes an episode—and for this reason loses significance. But it is intrinsically different as well: it does not function as a miracle in the fairy tale. Whereas in the saint's legend and in the local legend people are frightened or at least surprised when animals suddenly begin to speak, just the reverse is true in the fairy tale. The wild beast in the forest may frighten the fairy-tale hero, but as soon as it begins to speak, the anxiety vanishes. And even though in a few such cases the fairy-tale hero says, "What? You can speak?," this is no longer genuine fairy-tale style. The real fairy-tale hero is not astonished by miracles and magic; he accepts them as if they were a matter of course. Supernatural figures endowed with magical powers appear, to oppose or help him, not to bear witness for a completely different, supernatural world which makes us shudder in horror or ecstasy. The miracle is the vital substance in the fairy tale; it permeates the entire tale and is no longer told for its own sake. Compared with the fairy tale, the saint's legend and the local legend are relatively simple forms. They supply the fairy tale with building blocks; but in the hands of the fairy tale, these stones lose their weight. The fairy tale transforms them, plays with them, weaves them into a larger and greater whole which we experience in a completely different way than we do a local legend or a saint's legend: we experience the fairy tale as a work of art. Its characteristic style will be the subject of the next section.

CHAPTER 3

THE DRAGON SLAYER

The Style
of the Fairy Tale

The wonderful phrase "Once upon a time" is found not only in German fairy tales; all European peoples know and love it. "Once there was, One day there will be: this is the beginning of every fairy tale. There is no 'if' and no 'perhaps,' the three-legged stool unquestionably has three legs." These are the introductory words of a Breton tale, and they contain a brief statement of fairy-tale philosophy: "Once there was, One day there will be." The Breton narrator understands perfectly: the phrase *"Es war einmal"* by no means is intended to stress the fact that events in the tale took place in the past. The intent is to suggest the very opposite: what once occurred, has the tendency continually to recur. The ancient incantations liked to refer first to a former situation wherein the gods, demons, or saints being implored actually did help. Thus, they will now help again. What once happened will happen again and again. The Breton continues, "There is no 'if' and no 'perhaps,' the three-legged stool unquestionably has three legs." With this, he humorously alludes to the certainty and precision with which the fairy tale portrays its world. This certainty and sharpness is a basic characteristic found in all European fairy tales. The fairy-tale genre has its own style, which is clearly visible despite the individual and national characteristics of the narrative, from which a good portion of the fairy tale's charm emanates. In order to define this style more closely, we turn to the fairy tale of the dragon slayer.

The battle with the dragon—which at once reminds us of Siegfried and Perseus or St. George and the archangel Michael—is found in many folk tales as an episode in the fairy tale of the two brothers. Two brothers of miraculous birth grow up and go out into the world together. In some manner, they acquire as escorts beasts with supernatural powers—these are often three dogs, but sometimes a bear, a wolf, and a lion, or perhaps just one of these animals. Now the brothers part; but if something should happen to one of them, the other will learn of it by a certain sign: a knife that suddenly rusts, a tree that withers up, or a spring that becomes turbid. The following passage is taken from a Swedish variant of the fairy tale of the two brothers recorded more than 100 years ago, and tells how the story continues. The two brothers are here called Silberweiss and Lillwacker.

Silberweiss, alone, continued on his journey over high mountains and through deep valleys until he caught sight of a great city. But in the city all the houses were draped in black and the inhabitants walked about silently and sadly, as if there had been a great misfortune. Silberweiss entered town and inquired about the cause of all this sadness. The people said, "You must indeed come from far away, since you have not heard how the king and queen were in distress on the sea and were forced to promise their three daughters in marriage. Tomorrow the sea troll is to come and fetch the eldest princess." On hearing that, the youth became happy and thought what a fine opportunity that was to gain fame and fortune, if only his luck was favorable.

When morning came, Silberweiss buckled on his sword, called to his dogs and walked down to the seashore with them. Now as he was sitting there he saw the king's daughter coming from the city with a courtier, who had promised to save her. The princess, however, was very sad and cried bitterly. Now Silberweiss approached and greeted the beautiful maiden, but both she and her companion were greatly frightened at seeing him, since they thought him to be the sea troll. The courtier fled in great fear and hid in a tree which stood close by the sea. When Silberweiss saw how frightened she was, he said, "Beautiful maiden, do not fear me, for I will not cause you any harm." The princess answered, "Are you not the one who is coming to fetch me?"

"No," said Silberweiss, "I have come here to save you." When the princess heard this, she was very pleased that she had such a brave champion to fight for her and they had a long and friendly talk together. While they were talking, Silberweiss asked the princess to do him a favor and delouse him. The princess consented, and Silberweiss laid his head in her lap. And while he was resting there, the princess secretly took a gold ring from her finger and tied it on tightly with the youth's curly hair.

Suddenly the sea troll came up from the depths of the sea, churning the water into foam and waves all around him. When the troll saw Silberweiss, he became angry and said, "Why are you sitting there with my princess?" The youth answered, "I think she is more my princess than yours." The sea troll replied, "We shall see about that. But first our dogs must fight each other." Silberweiss agreed, ordered his dogs to attack the troll's dogs, and there was a great fight. Finally, the youth's dogs gained the upper hand and bit the troll's dogs to death. Then, Silberweiss drew his sword, walked up to the sea troll and dealt him such a mighty blow that the monster's head was severed and fell onto the sand. The troll emitted a dreadful scream and headed out to sea so fast that the water surged up to the clouds in the sky. The youth took his silver-handled knife, cut the troll's eyeballs out of its head and concealed them on his person. Then he greeted the beautiful princess and quickly went his way.

How is this fairy tale told? The first thing which strikes us is that there is nowhere a detailed description. We are given absolutely no idea how the sea monster looks (here called "a troll," the Scandinavian name). And yet a description of the monster is just what is expected at this point. For at first, not even the princess knows what a troll looks like, of course: she believes her rescuer Silberweiss to be the troll. Then, when the troll really

does appear, one would expect a description of him. But for the
purpose of the fairy tale, the word "monster" suffices. The sea and
the shore are likewise not described; not until the troll shoots up
out of the water does one see the foam and the waves churning
about. The fairy tale indicates the action and does not get lost in
the portrayal of scenes and characters. In how many so-called
"literary" fairy tales is a city which the hero enters lovingly described: the narrow streets, the picturesque corners and gables,
and the murmuring fountains? In the genuine fairy tale, there is
nothing of the sort. The only thing mentioned here—because it
has to do with the action—is that the houses are draped in black.
In other variants it reads: "painted black." This is just the opposite of an individualizing characterization; the houses lose their
distinctive character, and the city stands before us in abstract
stylization, so to speak. When the Grimm brothers tell of a witch's
long crooked nose or her red eyes, that is usually a little ornamentation of their own. The real fairy tale says only: an old witch, or
an ugly old woman. Nor does it describe the forest. "He entered a
great forest" is a set phrase in the fairy tale, which tells of flowers,
animals, and journeys only when they become important to the
plot. This absence of all desire to describe unessential details
gives the European fairy tale its clarity and precision. Its hero
moves and acts, he does not stand still in astonishment, contem-
plation, or meditation. A number of other things contribute to
this delightful clarity; for example, the mere isolation of the
characters. The two brothers separate; the princess approaches
the seashore with a single escort, and he, too, retreats when he
sees Silberweiss, so that the hero and the maiden face each other
alone. In addition, both characters stand out in themselves and
are raised above the multitude: she is a princess, he of miraculous
birth (his mother was a princess who became pregnant from
eating an apple). The fairy tale takes its heroes from the remotest
branches of society: the prince and the young swine herd, the
despised youngest son or the clumsy boy; and the girl who
watches the hearth or tends the geese and the princess. The fairy
tale is also fond of other extremes and contrasts: dreadful punish-
ments and splendid rewards, giants and dwarfs, mangy skull and

golden hair, good and evil, handsome and ugly, black and white. Thus, the fairy tale portrays a clearly and neatly fashioned world. It is fond of gold and silver not only because they shine and are rare and costly, and thereby clearly stand out from the multitude, like the prince or the girl who tends geese; it is fond of gold and silver, and iron and crystal, if for no other reason than that it prefers everything solid and clearly formed. The fairy tale tells of copper forests, glass implements, and wooden skirts. The very fact that it prefers castle and city to village and cave shows its predilection for what has been formed and created by the mind of man. It is no mere chance that the ring, sword, and knife are named in the short passage just quoted from the Swedish fairy tale about the dragon slayer. Such sharply defined objects occur in every fairy tale. Just as the course of the action is clear and unerring, the people and objects, too, are sharply outlined. And if the appearance of the characters is not described in detail, their inner feelings, as well, are not portrayed at any length. But they become outwardly visible, so to speak. The relationship of the princess to her deliverer is concretized in the ring which she ties into his hair, and even before that in his allowing her to delouse him. By no means is it necessary to know that delousing was a popular and necessary activity among primitive peoples and that it could also be an engagement ceremony in which the woman would eat the lice, thus absorbing the partner's blood. It is not at all necessary to think of these things, and yet one senses, nevertheless, that these actions symbolize making a connection. In the fairy tale, feelings and relationships are externalized, sometimes in a manner which for us is quite peculiar, as in the tale just mentioned. All these things we have observed, however, produce a similar effect. The steady progression of the action, the dispensing with a detailed portrayal of the background or the characters, the predilection for everything clearly formed (in colors as well as in shape), the tendency toward extremes and contrasts, toward metals and minerals, cities, castles, rooms, boxes, rings, and swords, and the tendency to make feelings and relationships congeal into objects, so to speak, and thus become outwardly visible—all these things give the fairy tale definiteness, firmness, clarity. The fairy tale bestows on its hearer, without him being aware of it, something of its unaffected precision and brilliance.

How does our Swedish fairy tale continue? Silberweiss rescues the second princess and, finally, the third one as well.

On the third day Silberweiss buckled on his sword, called to his three dogs and went back down to the sea. As he sat on the beach he saw the youngest princess coming from the city and with her the brave courtier whom everyone believed to be her sisters' deliverer. The princess, however, was very sad and cried bitterly. Now Silberweiss approached her and politely greeted the beautiful maiden. When the princess and her escort caught sight of the good-looking young man they were terribly startled, for they believed him to be the sea troll. The courtier ran away and hid in a tall tree near the shore. When Silberweiss noticed how frightened she was, he said, "Beautiful maiden, do not be afraid of me, for I will do you no harm." The princess answered, "Are you not the one who has come to take me away?" "No," said Silberweiss, "I have come here to free you." When the princess heard this, she was delighted that such a brave warrior wanted to fight for her, and they had a long and friendly talk together. And while they were talking, Silberwesis asked the beautiful maiden to do him a favor and delouse him. The princess gladly complied with his wish, and Silberweiss laid his head in her lap. Now the princess was surprised to see the golden rings which her sisters had tied in the youth's hair, and without him noticing it she tied yet another ring in his locks.

Suddenly the sea troll emerged from the depths with a great roar, so that the waves and sea spray rose up to the sky. But now he had six heads and nine dogs. When the troll saw Silberweiss sitting with the young princess he became angry and cried out, "What are you doing there next to my princess?" The youth answered, "I think she is more my princess than yours." The troll replied, "We shall see. But first our dogs must fight together." Silberweiss did not have to be told twice—he ordered his dogs to attack the sea dogs and there was a violent struggle. But in the end, the youth's dogs won out and bit all nine sea dogs to death. And Silberweiss drew his gleaming sword, stepped right up to the sea troll and slashed away until all six heads rolled onto the sand. The monster let out a dreadful shriek and headed out to sea so that the water surged up toward the clouds. Then Silberweiss took his silver-handled knife and cut the twelve eyeballs out of the troll's heads. He greeted the princess and quickly went his way.

Our hero's third act of rescue is described in almost the same words as the first. Here, we come upon a further basic characteristic of the fairy tale: its delight in repetition. It is a peculiarity of the Swedish tale and some other northern European versions that there are three princesses to be saved. For the remainder of the story, that is not exactly an advantage, for despite the three rings in his hair, the hero can of course marry only *one* of the princesses —the youngest, naturally. His brother Lillwacker will then court the second oldest; and the oldest princess is not even mentioned again. Despite such drawbacks, the fairy tale cannot resist its innate propensity for repetition. The fact that there are three princesses, three sea dragons, three battles, and three dogs who come to the rescue is a result of the fairy tale's partiality for certain set numbers: three, seven, twelve, one hundred. This partiality for round numbers is in keeping with the fairy tale's previously observed striving for preciseness. But in addition to the number three, the almost word-for-word repetition conforms very closely to the rigid style of the fairy tale. We must not blame it on the clumsiness of the teller. It is the fairy tale's own innate stylistic urge for rigidity of form through repetition. In comparing fairy tale, local legend, and saint's legend, we observed that the two kinds of legend have a feeling for time and the passage of time, whereas the fairy tale seems to portray a timeless world. In so doing, we by no means place a negative evaluation on the fairy tale. The poetic art of the fairy tale does not concern transient things; it portrays an imperishable, eternal world. The troll's eyes and the dragon's tongue, which in most variants of the dragon-killer story are cut out and then, a year later, replaced, are absolute characteristics not subject to the effects of time. The same changelessness is expressed in the inflexible repetitions of entire sentences, indeed whole sections, found in the tales of all peoples side by side with a delight in variation and poetic inventiveness. In so doing, psychological improbabilities are casually tolerated. It is perhaps conceivable that the younger sister also considered

Silberweiss to be the troll; but it is not believable that the courtier, as well, thinks this to be the case. Here the stylistic law of the fairy tale again shows its effect: it not only isolates the figures; to a considerable extent it also isolates the episodes. Each one is complete within itself; the relation to the earlier episode need not be established. This technique of isolation contributes to the sharply defined structure of the fairy tale and intensifies the severity of the fairy-tale style. The word-for-word repetition can impart to it something almost sacral, and it is a basic error of editors and translators to attempt here and there to introduce qualifications and nuances in order to spare the modern reader. Just recently we have acquired a new feeling for the sacral, the stylized, the abstract. The repetitions in the fairy tale are ornamentation, a basic part of its style. We can also infer from our text that within this great urge for repetition there is also room for certain variations—which, to be sure, are likewise stylized: the first troll has one head, the second has three, and the third six. Here, we encounter the tendency toward stylized intensification well known to every fairy-tale hearer: the last adventure is the most dangerous, the youngest princess the most beautiful, the youngest son is the fairy-tale hero. And something more—the teller does not forget the two rings in Silberweiss's hair when it becomes the youngest princess's turn to tie her ring into the same locks. This shows that the fairy-tale episodes are not completely sealed off from each other, after all. Tendencies toward repetition and variation, toward self-sufficiency of the individual scene and integrated structure, stand in opposition to each other, but do so in such a way that isolation and repetition manifest themselves more strongly than we are used to in individual literature.

The fairy tale of the two brothers now goes on to tell how the false courtier, king's counselor, colonel, coachman, or charcoal burner claims to be the slayer of the dragon or the troll, and forces the princess—in most variants there is only one—to be silent. She has to marry him, but begs the king for a year's grace, and he grants her request. In exactly one year the real hero returns, and by means of the identifying objects, unmasks the pretender. He marries the princess, but is later outwitted and killed by demonic powers, usually relatives of the slain dragon. Now his brother notices the sign telling of his death, and starts out to search for him. He finds him and is able to revive him. These later parts of the fairy tale of the two brothers do not concern us here. Let us in conclusion turn our attention instead to the return of the dragon slayer a year later. This time our example is taken from an Austrian tale recorded in the province of Styria in 1916.

> And amid the festivities the year passed in no time; one more day and the princess was to become the charcoal burner's wife. On the day before the wedding, the fisherman's son and his four animals returned to the same inn he had stayed in before, and learned from the innkeeper that on the following day the wedding of the princess and the charcoal burner who had killed the dragon was to take place.
>
> "Well, well!" drawled Sepp, and yawned, "that's news to me," then went to bed.
>
> But the next morning he asked the innkeeper, "I wonder what will be served at the wedding feast? I would really like a piece of the roast." And he borrowed a little basket, wrote a note and put it in. He then put the handle in his dog's mouth, and at once the dog ran off down the street. It ran past all the guards into the castle and right up to the grieving princess. But when she saw the dog she burst out laughing for joy, led the dog into the kitchen and put a large piece from the wedding roast in the basket. The dog then ran straight back to the inn.
>
> "Now we have some of the wedding roast," Sepp said, taking the little basket out of the dog's mouth, "but I wonder how the wine is? I would really like a little bottle of it." So he put the little basket in the bear's mouth, put a note and a bottle in the basket, and the bear knew what to do. It ran growling through the narrow streets and slipped past all the palace guards, until it stood in front of the princess. She laughed even more joyfully when she caught sight of the bear. She took the little bottle and the note, filled the bottle with fine wine and dismissed the bear, which trotted straight back to the inn.
>
> "Why, I still am lacking the pudding," cried the guest, while the innkeeper stood gaping in astonishment. "I must have that,

CHAPTER 4

THE USES
OF FAIRY TALES

Cinderella

Hansel and Gretel

The White Snake

What is there about the folk fairy tale that has such a strange fascination? "Sleeping Beauty," "Snow White," "Hansel and Gretel," "The Seven Ravens"—one need mention only a few titles to stir up memories. Yet these tales concern themselves not with just happiness and light, but quite often wih privation and suffering, cruelty and betrayal, murder and death. The charm of the fairy tale is explained not only by the fact that everything usually comes out all right in the end—for the hero or heroine at least—or that the good people are rewarded and the bad ones punished. It is more than mere wish-fulfillment literature. The religious historian Mircea Eliade once said that the hearers of fairy tales, without being aware of it, experience a sort of initiation not entirely unlike that in the customs of some primitive peoples. "The folk fairy tale transposes the initiation process into the sphere of imagination. . . . Without rendering account to ourselves but rather in the full belief that we are merely relaxing and being entertained, modern man too enjoys the imaginative initiation that the fairy tale affords us." How correct this scholar's assertion is can be shown in any folk fairy tale. It is not surprising that it becomes especially clear in the best known, most popular tales.

Cinderella

The fairy tale of Cinderella has spread over half the world in many different versions. It is familiar to us from the Grimm brothers. "You tame pigeons, you turtledoves, all you birds under the heavens, come and help me pick them out,/the good ones in the pot,/the bad ones in your crop." And the birds come and pick out all the lentils that the wicked stepmother had poured in the ashes, separating the good ones from the bad. But the stepmother still won't let the child go to the king's party, although with the help of the doves she has twice completed the task given to her by the malicious stepmother; and so the child goes "to her mother's grave underneath the hazel tree: 'Little tree shiver and shake, Scatter gold and silver over me.'" And she receives clothes of silver and gold. This brief section at once makes visible the basic situation: Cinderella, rejected by people, receives help from the animals and a tree. Human society, even the family, appears as an enemy, nature as a friend. The child who hears this story feels: "No matter how much I may be slighted by others, I can trust in stronger and kinder forces." In other fairy tales, the heroine is given presents by the stars; here, it is the birds and a hazel tree: that is, nature and the cosmic forces surrounding us protect and sustain us.

The helping animal and helping tree are joined by a third helping power: the love of the deceased mother. Even if our immediate human surroundings forsake us or torment us, we are still not dependent on the mercy of nature alone; human care and human warmth that was once present continues to have an invisible effect. In some tales related to the Cinderella story, man and nature are even more closely intertwined than they are here. If a little bird on the mother's grave can be construed as the embodiment of the deceased mother's soul—in the belief of some primitive peoples, birds are soul animals—it is easy to see maternal forces at work in the helping doves. Likewise, there is a whole group of fairy tales in which the helping animal—usually a little cow or goat, clearly a metamorphic form of the deceased mother —provides the tormented girl with food and clothing. The deceased in the fairy tale are not ghostly, like those in the local legend, but enter into the play of forces; the realm of plants, animals, and the deceased embodied in the hazel tree, the doves, and the mother render their friendly assistance to helpless man in the Cinderella fairy tale.

Cinderella is helpless, forsaken, and alone, like so many other heroes and heroines in the fairy tale; and in the many other versions, we see her cry even more often than in Grimm. Crying, the sign of helplessness, summons assistance—again a feature recurring in innumerable fairy tales. Precisely as an outcast can man hope to find help.

The fairy tale is an initiation. Man is cast into suffering and want, evidently destined to endure privation, misunderstanding, and malice, and yet summoned to a regal existence. Man is surrounded by hostile and helping forces; but he is not entirely at their mercy: through his own attitude—perseverance, humility, and trust—he can be supported through the help of nature and the enduring, strengthening love of the deceased mother and can thus be led to the light. The ashen color, the dirt and dust which cling to the girl, are not mere signs of her life as a kitchen maid; they are, as suggested by many similar features in fairy tales and myths of all times and peoples, at the same time signs of her relationship to a higher, supernatural world. Cinderella is closely related to the realm of the dead, and she bears its mark. But even though the Cinderella tale, in a profound sense, provides a sort of initiation, an imaginative introduction for the listener into the real nature of his existence, on the surface many other things are involved. For example, the problem of semblance and reality: the insignificant thing turns out to be glorious; the dirty child is mere disguise; the clothes of silver and gold finally reveal the true nature of the girl who wears them. Thus, we find the separation of good and evil, of true and false; not only are the evil characters unmasked and condemned at the end, but even before that the theme of separating, judging, and arranging is present in the motif of the sorting out of the lentils (or, in other variants, the beans, peas, or grains of wheat): "The good ones in the pot, the bad ones in your crop." In the Grimm version the wicked step-mother pours the lentils in the ashes; in other variants, it is clearer that the essential point is the separation of the good seeds from the bad. In addition, the tale—still on the surface—has the engaging, warm, and sentimental tendency to praise diligence, neatness, and cleanliness (which also stands for chastity) and to castigate the jealousy, malice, and laziness of the stepsisters. Finally, traces of the wish-fulfilling dream and even of desire for vengeance are present.

The cruel punishment of the two stepsisters in the Grimm version is rather shocking. Without the slightest protest on the part of Cinderella, the doves peck out the eyes of the wicked sisters—hardly what we would expect from these creatures, which are usually symbols of gentleness. There is a detailed description of how they peck one eye out of each sister on the way to church and the other eye on the way back. One constantly hears objections to telling such stories to children, and rightly so. However, the Grimm version is internally consistent. The mutilation of the two stepsisters is in a way the answer to their self-mutilation: they cut off their toe and heel, and then their eyes are taken from them by the forces of retribution; what they themselves began is completed from above. But there is great danger that this process, which, taken symbolically, has its justification, may be understood too literally. In telling the story it is all right for us to leave out this episode, all the more so since it did not even appear in the first edition of *Grimm's Fairy Tales*. In a Hungarian-German variant and in the classical French fairy-tale book of Perrault—where we must, however, make allowances for the latter's irony—the wicked sisters are expressly forgiven. "Cinderella was as kind-hearted as she was beautiful," says Perrault (1697). "She received her sisters in the palace and on the same day had them married to two noblemen at the king's court." And in a version told in our

own century among German-speaking people in Hungary, reported by Elli Zenker-Starzacher: "Before they left she went to her
mother and her sisters and told them they should reflect on all the
things they had done to her. But she wasn't angry at them; she
forgave them everything; and she hoped that God would forgive
them too. And they bade them adieu and were gone." The
Neapolitan Basile choose a middle course (1634): "Livid with
envy and unable to deaden the pain in their hearts, the daughters
of Carmosina slinked silently and furtively back into their
mother's house." However, he adds that this punishment seemed
too mild to many people: "There was no punishment that their
haughtiness did not deserve and no penalty befitting their envy."
Thus, the various needs of the times and of individual people are
reflected in the styles of the storytellers and in the reactions of the
hearers. "The fairy tale has no landlord" is a common expression
in Greece. Each storyteller can tell it in his own way, so long as he
faithfully retains the basic structure, and, thus, the essential details with their deeper meaning not easily comprehended by
reason. The language of *Grimm's Fairy Tales* is so charming and
poetic that we would like to consider these tales sacrosanct; however, in the case of Cinderella, we may change the ending without
any harm.

Hansel and Gretel

The story of Hansel and Gretel—like Little Red Riding Hood,
the Seven Does, Tom Thumb, and others—is one of a group of
children's fary tales, so called because children are the principal
characters in them.

A child has a natural right to be protected and cared for. It is
said of Little Red Riding Hood that everyone who saw her liked
her, and the grandmother "simply couldn't think of anything else
she might give the child." Hansel and Gretel, however, are cast
out by their parents. In the fairy tale of Snow White, jealousy is
the root of evil; in the story of Hansel and Gretel, as we find it in

Grimm and Bechstein, poverty provides the basis for the hardness of heart. The parents are poor, and finally they can "no longer get their daily bread." This brings out the mother's cruel nature: she thinks of herself first, rather than the children, and she wants to be rid of them. The man resists for a while, but "she allowed him no rest until he agreed."

The folk fairy tale knows that poverty and deprivation ordinarily do not make man better, but rather worse; or, more precisely, they prepare the ground for evil. The fairy tale differentiates, too, between father and mother. In "The Twelve Brothers" and related tales, the father wishes to kill his sons, and the mother wishes to protect them; here, however, it is the father who protests. But he is weak, as in a remarkable number of other fairy tales, and here, too, finally yields to the strong will of his wife. The mother or stepmother rejects the children and wants to let them die of hunger so that she herself won't have to go hungry; the witch does exactly the reverse, luring the children to her in order to have a good meal. Concern for their daily bread dehumanizes the parents; the witch's gluttony has the effect of a grotesque echo. Thus, we are constantly amazed by the fairy tale's artistic capability to sustain and vary a theme.

Even more clearly than in the case of the evil queen in "Snow White," the witch in Hansel and Gretel is not a person, but a mere figure, a personification of evil. And more clearly than in "Snow White," where the evil queen has to dance herself to death, the witch perishes by her own devices. She suffers the fate she had intended for the children: she is roasted in her own oven, she dies by a method she herself had invented. Evil consumes itself. It is striking how frequently and persistently the folk fairy tale depicts this phenomenon. It is to be found in one figure or another in almost every tale.

Psychological investigators of the fairy tale claim to see in the witch an image of the destructive power of the unconscious. The same is said of the stepmother. "That the latter has also died after the destruction of the witch," one reads in Hedwig von Beit's and Marie-Louise von Franz' *The Symbolism of Fairy Tales*, "proves the secret identity of the two women." We beg to differ;

this identity is by no means proven. Even though a number of things suggest it, we cannot say it is certain. The danger of all symbolic fairy-tale interpretation is that it is too hasty in regarding its hypotheses as proven. C. G. Jung and his school consider the most significant achievement of the fairy tale to be the depiction of processes within the soul. An interesting and fruitful theory—but whether it is correct cannot be proved; at best, it can only be established as probable. Opinions can differ on whether the witch is really an aspect of the unconscious. On the other hand, it is clear enough that she is a manifestation of evil and that she perishes by her own devices.

Hansel and Gretel are more active than the usual fairy-tale heroes. They eavesdrop on their parents; Hansel discovers a method to find the way back home and thus to thwart the scheme the first time. Then he succeeds several times in deceiving the witch. When his resources no longer suffice, the sister becomes active and outwits the witch. Thereupon, in the first edition of *Grimm's Fairy Tales*, the children find their way home alone; only later is the episode added in which a duck carries them across the water. Hence, the helping animal that we are familiar with in so many other fairy tales also appears in this story. Most fairy tales do not have children but rather a youth or a maiden as the hero or heroine. And they generally must depend on the advice, help, and often the gifts of supernatural beings.

Thus, it is noteworthy that Hansel and Gretel manage to do without outside help completely in the first printed version, and that even in the later form the helping animal has only a small role. A look at other children's fairy tales will show us that this astonishing independence on the part of the child is no exception. In Tom Thumb stories, the youngest and smallest brother—that is, Tom Thumb himself—is by far the sliest of all.

Thus, children in fairy tales are by no means helpless; many of them free themselves by their own ability and cunning. The fairy tale shows not only that children have need of care and protection, it also gives them the ingenuity to make their way and to save themselves. In contrast to the older, adolescent heroes in the fairy tale, Hansel and Gretel do not venture forth happily into the world, but attempt to return home. Yet the child, no matter how much it depends on the care of grownups, is surer of himself than the adolescent, whose dependence on mental and spiritual help is reflected in the dependence of fairy-tale heroes on gifts from supernatural beings.

A knowledge of the variants and parallels to "Hansel and Gretel" keeps us from making false, or one-sided, judgments. The story "The Children in the House of the Monster" is known all over the world. The monster can be a male ogre just as well as a witch; sometimes, as for example in an Indian folk tale, they are man and wife, in which case the male cannibal usually has a more avid and relentless craving for children's flesh. We must therefore not be misled to hasty conclusions by the fact that, in "Hansel and Gretel," the mother is harsher and the monster a female witch.

All these stories reflect the threat to the child of mysterious forces, as well as the child's ability to master these forces. In a number of variants, some of the brothers or sisters fall victim to the devouring monsters; but those who get away unscathed come out of the conflict enriched: Hansel and Gretel bring home pearls and jewels. Those who are exposed to danger can naturally perish in it; but they can also grow in it. Fairy tales present both pos- sibilities, metaphorically and highly stylized, to our mind's eye.

Several years ago, Hans Traxler, in an amusing parody of archeological methods, asserted his intention to trace the fairy tale of Hansel and Gretel back to its true origins. His delightfully written book, *Die Wahrheit über Hänsel und Gretel*, led a lot of people on a wild goose chase and created considerable confusion. Actually, the real origins are not the important thing in the fairy tale. It is quite likely that behind many features in our fairy tales there are old customs and beliefs; but in the context of the tale, they have lost their original character. Fairy tales are experienced by their hearers and readers, not as realistic, but as symbolic poetry.

The White Snake

When grownups think back to fairy tales heard in their childhood, they can often only remember a single image that still stands out, while having forgotten the entire context. It is not necessarily the picture that an illustrator has taken from the story: even without such assistance, a certain feature in the fairy tale may especially impress the hearer and stay with him as an image for the rest of his life.

In Grimm's fairy tale, "The White Snake," a youth rides forth into the world; one day an entire colony of ants crawls across his path, and the youth hears the ant king lament the fact that "his people" will be crushed to death. The youth leads his horse into a side road so that the heavy hoofs will not harm the ants. "We will repay you," cries the ant king, as the youth rides off. Anyone who has heard or read this incident in his childhood and has been receptive to it, will forever have a different attitude toward the living creatures around him than the person who has grown up without such influence. It is not only the real world that has an effect on us; the story-book world, with its invisible images, is absorbed by our mind more easily and imperceptibly; this world is preformed and predestined to enter the treasury of our imagination and thus to take part in the building of our world view.

The title "The White Snake" is explained by the events at the beginning of the fairy tale: the youth takes a taste of a little piece of meat in a covered bowl on the king's table. The meat comes from a white snake, and from then on the youth understands the speech of the animals. He hears not only the lament of the ant king, but also that of fish stranded in low water and young ravens that have been thrown out of their nest. And he helps them all. Thus one image follows the other; but the fairy tale does not merely string these images together: they fit together in a meaningful chain of events. The early scenes tell how the young servant acquires knowledge of the language of animals and requests a horse from the king. This introduction is not absolutely necessary. In other fairy tales, the hero or heroine understands what the animals say without any detailed explanation of how this is done. But the image of the covered bowl containing a white snake is quite striking and easily remembered. This clear portrayal of objects together with their mysterious, unaccountable properties is characteristic of fairy-tale style. This aspect we find repeated in Kafka's stories, which, for other reasons, have been given the name "anti-fairy tales."

It is an old wish-dream of man to comprehend the language of the animals. The lucky fellow in the fairy tale has this wish fulfilled in a simple and effortless manner, an anticipation in the fairy tale of a scientific goal which, in a different way, has again been fascinating and occupying us for several decades. More significant, however, is the continuation of the story: the youth has "the desire to see the world." We soon note that it is not a matter of a casual sightseeing trip; first, the youth on horseback takes pity on the various animals and, afterward, feels called upon to accomplish difficult tasks and to win the hand of the princess. This is a pattern that recurs in innumerable fairy tales: the man sets forth into the unknown in search of the highest, the most beautiful, or the most valuable thing. He is set tasks which seem unsolvable, but help comes to him. In our story, the three fish he has saved get him the golden ring from the bottom of the ocean, the ants pick the millet seeds out of the grass for him, and the three ravens bring him the golden apple of life from the end of the world—the final wish of the princess. Each time—and this is characteristic not only of our fairy tale, but recurs in many others in a similar way—the hero is at a loss; he sits down sadly and has no hope of being able to solve the task. He doesn't think of the animals he has helped, even after he has twice received their aid. He is not aware of his possibilities. He has not helped the animals in order to derive benefit from it, but for just this reason they are able to help him. Without being aware of it, he has developed powers within himself which can now sustain him. The abilities of the grown animals correspond exactly to the tasks confronting him. Two important and basic features of the European folk fairy tale become visible here: the abstract yet precise interrelationship of things and the tendency toward isolation. The hero wanders forth from his familar surroundings, he isolates himself; yet at the same time he encounters other animals and people and establishes contact with them. This is *the* image of man which somehow shines forth in every fairy tale: outwardly isolated, but for just this reason free to establish essential contacts. The fact that the hero of our fairy tale each time despairs anew of solving his task is a further effect on the fairy tale's isolating style: the fairy-tale hero is unable to see a pattern in his experiences—he repeatedly finds himself in a similar difficult situation; and then from nowhere, so it seems, the help appears. The helper, however, as our fairy tale and others of the same type show especially clearly, is somehow part of him. Without his own knowledge and without intending to, the youth himself has created the preconditions for the aid. The fact that he is not aware of this is expressed in many tales. At the same time, there are others in which he demands his reward. The hero of Grimm's "The Sea-hare," who has to hide so that he cannot be found in order to win the hand of the princess, goes straight to the raven in the forest, to the fish in the lake, and to the fox in the field, and says each time: "I spared your life; now tell me where I may hide so that the princess will not see me!" The fish hides him in an egg, the raven in its stomach, but both times the princess discovers him, even though not until she has looked through the eleventh and the twelfth windows. The fox finally transforms the youth—the hundredth one to take up the princess's challenge—into a sea-hare which hides under the princess's braid. Now she cannot find him. In other variants, the hero is transformed by the helper into a flea that hides in the princess's robe, an apple that she puts in her pocket, or a rosemary leaf that gets into her ear. A well-known and basic theme finds expression here: man knows everything better than he knows himself. The sharp-eyed princess discovers the youth wherever he hides: whether it be below or above the earth, at the bottom of the sea or up in a tree, but she cannot see herself.

In the story of the white snake, as in the stylistically somewhat different tale of the sea-hare, the hero comes in contact with beasts of the earth, the water, and the air: he partakes of all three realms. The European folk fairy tale has this tendency to be universal. The hero sets forth and discovers the relationship to entirely different spheres. This, too, is a motif that makes a deep impression on the hearer, for it appears over and over in the most diverse fairy tales. Most often animals are involved, which the hero aids and which in turn help him. Fairy-tale researchers speak of the "helping animal" or the "grateful animal," terms used by the Grimm brothers and also employed specifically in our tale of "The White Snake." As we have indicated, the animals can be viewed as forces within the soul of the individual which are at first in need of assistance but finally unfold and develop. But beyond this, all these stories also reflect the relationship of man to real animals. Man is in contact with nature, which accepts his assistance and in turn comes to his aid. It is not mere coincidence that so many helpers in the fairy tale are animals.

It may be disturbing that in the same tale of "The White Snake," the hero kills his horse without a moment's hesitation in order to feed the three young ravens. This is an expression of the isolating technique in the fairy tale. The ravens are here the focus of interest, not the horse, thus it can be readily sacrificed. In addition there is the fact that it is a real sacrifice: from then on the youth must go on foot. This is significant in the framework of the story; the horse itself is of little consequence. Anyone familiar with the isolating technique of the fairy tale—something entirely in harmony with the spirit of the child—is not surprised that the hero's sympathy is evoked by the ants, the fish, and the raven, but not by his own horse. The white snake is also not spared, as we know: it is only a means by which man learns the language of the animals.

The handsome youth set out to see the world, but at once demands are made on him and, later, he steps forward to solve the difficult tasks. This course, or one similar to it, is followed in most fairy tales. It corresponds to the course followed by the maturing or matured human being throughout life. Fairy tales are unreal but they are not untrue; they reflect essential developments and conditions of man's existence.

CHAPTER 5

THE LITTLE EARTH-COW

Symbolism in the Fairy Tale

There are different ways to tell fairy tales, and each has its own charm. Years ago, when the fairy tale was a part of the evening's entertainment in the villages, one could hear some storytellers who embellished their tales and others who gave concise and forceful accounts. Some changed the story each time they told it, and others kept the same wording intact, as if the words were sacred and inviolable—and both versions were acclaimed. The kindly, maternal tone of voice which awakens a child's love and understanding for fairy tales is in its way just as well received as the mysterious, magical tone which carries the spellbound listener off into another world.

Also, in regard to the contents, the tales conform to the character and imaginative faculty of the various storytellers. The Spanish shepherd who is given a magic fife makes his sheep dance; but the goatherd from the canton of Grisons has his goats line up for close-order drill. He orders them to stand up on their hind legs, dresses the ranks, and has them march like this into the village. Later, he even cuts sticks for the goats, which he makes them hold up between their forelegs like rifles. While here the military tradition of the Swiss intrudes upon the fairy tale, the democratic custom is conspicuous in another tale from Grisons. In this version of the Snow White tale, the beautiful maiden repeatedly ignores the orders of the dwarfs, buys something from the disguised stepmother, and even lets her in the room. When the dwarfs notice this, they lose their patience. "They were very angry," it says, "and decided by vote of the majority whether or not they should fry the girl in the pan. But the majority was in favor of letting her live." Such national, regional, and individual characteristics are among the finest, liveliest, and merriest elements in fairy tales. But beneath the superficial dissimilarities, one detects a common style underlying all European fairy tales, which asserts itself time and again despite all the deviations and ornamentation. We have previously observed the fairy tale's love of action, clarity, precision, and compactness. The fairy-tale style can be illustrated in the story of the Little Earth-Cow, recorded during the sixteenth century in Alsace. The tale will also induce us to inquire into the significance of animals and symbolism in general in the fairy tale.

The Little Earth-Cow

A poor but good man had a wife and two little girls, the younger named Gretel and the older Anny, but before these children had grown up the mother died, and so he took another wife. Now she became jealous of Gretel and wished for the child's death, but didn't think it wise to kill the child herself. Thus, she cunningly enticed the older girl so that she would like her and hate her sister.

Now it happened one day that the mother and the older daughter were sitting together discussing just what to do in order to get rid of the maiden. They finally decided they would go to the forest together and take the little girl along. Then they would send her so far into the forest that she could not find her way back to them.

Now the little girl was standing outside the door and heard all the bad things that her mother and her sister were saying about her and how they were seeking her death; and she was very sad to have to die so miserably for no reason, and to be torn to pieces by the wolves. Thus, she went to her godmother and sadly told her of this great treachery and the deadly and murderous judgment of her sister and her mother. "Very well, now, my dear child," said the good old woman, "since this is the way things stand, go and get some sawdust and strew it on the ground as you walk behind your mother. And then, when they run away from you, just follow the trail of sawdust and you will find your way back home.

The little girl did what the old woman had told her. And when they got out in the forest, the mother sat down and said to the older girl, "Come here, Anny, and pick my lice. Meanwhile Gretel will go and fetch us three loads of wood. We shall wait here and then go home together."

The fairy tale is told in the ingenuous manner of sixteenth-century Germany. Diminutive syllables and adjectives give to it something childlike and intimate. But doom—envy, treachery, plans for murder—descends on this harmless world. The fairy tale, a short epic form, tends to embrace the entire world. Here, too, just as in the first section of "Sleeping Beauty," the basic motifs of human existence are present at the very outset: life and death; good and evil; temptation and intrigue; weakness and innocence; despair, guidance, and assistance. In addition, there are the spheres of the home and family, and nature—the forest and its animals. If the fairy tale is to incorporate the elements of existence in such a way, it must greatly simplify them. One means of accomplishing this is through intensification toward the extremes: a poor man, an old woman, a wicked stepmother. Dislike is expressed directly as lust for murder. Thus, the fairy tale's predilection for cruelty results from its attempt to give everything the clearest and sharpest possible form. This same tendency toward clarity is expressed in our tale in the manner in which everything is discussed between the various characters and is thus externalized. The wicked stepmother does not secretly contrive her murderous plan; it develops in the conversation with the older daughter and can thus be overheard by the younger one. The latter is also not alone in her grief and need not discover for herself the means of salvation: she gets the advice of her godmother. The characters in the fairy tale, as a rule, are guided less by their own decisions than by external impulses: advice, magic gifts, tasks, misfortunes. Thus, a clearly formed and conspicuous line of action develops. Close relationship between two people is revealed here, symbolized by the affectionate delousing of the scalp, just as in the Swedish fairy tale of the dragon slayer, which shows how widespread this ancient motif is. Hardly a trace can be detected of magical ideas, which in former times have been associated with this activity in the fairy tale. But the feature corresponds to the tendency of fairy tales to transform everything internal into something external, to portray the intimate relationship between two people in an image. Our fairy tale of the little earth-cow now tells how the poor little girl is led out into the forest a second and a third time. Each time the situation is exactly the same and is reported in almost the same words, so that the tale is divided up neatly in conformity with the basic style of the European fairy tale. The second time, at the suggestion of her godmother, good little Gretel takes chaff with her, and thus again finds her way home. But the third time she takes along hemp-seeds.

And when the poor girl wanted to go home she found that the birds had eaten up all the seeds. Alas, the poor little girl was so sad! All day she ran about in the forest, crying and calling out and telling God of her great sorrow. But she could not find the way out of the forest—in fact, she had gone further into it than any person ever before. When evening came, the poor, forlorn girl had nearly given up all hope, but she climbed a very high tree to see if she could not catch sight of some city, village or house where she might go so she would not come to a sad end as food for the wild beasts. And, indeed, in looking around she discovered a little column of smoke. She quickly descended and walked in the direction of the smoke, and in a few hours arrived at the place from which the smoke came. It was a tiny little house where nobody lived except an earth-cow. The little girl went to the door, knocked, and asked to be let in. The earth-cow answered, "I shall certainly not let you in unless you promise to spend your life here with me and never tell anyone about me and betray me." The little girl gave her promise and the earth cow immediately let her in. And the earth cow said, "Very well, all you need to do is milk me in the morning, and again in the evening. Then you may drink my milk and I will bring you silk and velvet to make all the pretty clothes your heart desires. But remember to be careful not to tell anyone about me! Even if your own sister should come to the door do not let her in and betray my presence here. If you do, I shall lose my life." After speaking these words, the earth-cow went to its pasture, and when it returned in the evening it brought silk and velvet from which the good, little Gretel made such pretty clothes that she could have stood comparison with a princess.

What do we imagine an earth-cow to be? No one knows exactly. Since related tales often speak of a cow that spins thread, or sometimes of a bull, we are probably dealing with a real cow here, as well: a sort of wild cow, not a deer or hind like the one we are familiar with in the Genoveva tale. In addition, the tale mentions the animal's horns, not antlers. On the other hand, a variant recorded in 1937 or 1938 in the German-speaking part of Lorraine tells of a deer which, despite its enormous antlers, is a dam. Thus, in the process of being handed down, the strange forest-cow has adapted to its milieu. Little "earth-men" in fairy tales are dwarfs; the name "Little Earth-Cow" accordingly may characterize the animal as a supernatural being. Ninon Hesse, in a reference to Vergil, establishes the relationship to Proserpina, the goddess of the underworld, to whom cows were sacrificed. In an Old English spell, a certain Erce is invoked as "mother of the earth," or goddess of the underworld. However, the interpretation of the word Erce (pronounced Erke) is not certain, and possibly it is not a name at all, but just an unintelligible magic word. The sixteenth century, and perhaps even Goethe—who alludes on one occasion to the fairy tale of the little earth-cow in a letter to Frau von Stein—may still have known exactly what was meant by it. This knowledge we have lost, but we hardly feel it to be a loss. The word which sounds so strange and yet at once familiar is right at home in the atmosphere of the fairy tale, which tells of strange things in the most matter-of-fact tone. It is as in modern poems, when an incomprehensible word or an inscrutable figure of speech at times speaks to us with great force and awakens very specific feelings. The little earth-cow that lives in a little house far off in the middle of the forest and can talk and dispense silk and velvet—no one tells us how—is welcomed and accepted without great surprise by the hearer of the tale almost as readily and gladly as it is by the good little Gretel. She is not in the least astonished that the little earth-cow can speak. As we have seen in our second chapter, the miracle is not a cause of wonderment in the fairy tale, as in the saint's legend. Rather, it is an essential element permeating all things; it is part of the fairy tale's vital substance. Everything can enter into relationship with everything else: that is the actual miracle and at the same time the simple foregone conclusion in the fairy tale. The little earth-cow can give its protégé not just milk, as is natural, but also such costly artificial things as silk and velvet. The deer in the Genoveva legend is portrayed far more realistically; it cannot speak, nor does it have a little house: it simply offers its milk to the outcast Genoveva and her child. This is the relatively realistic style of the saint's legend and the local legend. In the fairy tale, however, it is by no means an obsession with miracles but a profound stylistic necessity that places the earth-cow in a little house and has it dispense silk and velvet. Similarly, Rumpelstilskin lives in a little house, whereas the dwarf in a corresponding local legend dwells in a cave. Again, in place of the cave of Polyphemus in Homer, something far more constructive appears in analogous fairy tales: the man-eating monster lives in a palace. The cave, as it appears in the local legend, is not only more realistic, it also has less form. Castles, palaces, and little houses, with their vertical and horizontal lines, their steps, corridors, large halls, and little rooms, are conscious creations of the intellect—with abstract geometric sharpness, clarity, and purity. Thus, the stylistic necessities of the fairy tale—which we have observed in other instances —are manifested here, too, and over and over again. The greater the contrast, the sharper the portrayal: for this reason, the fairy tale tells of the princess and the swineherd; of the wedding feast and death by execution; and of a little earth-cow that provides silk and velvet and lives in a little house. In one of the familiar

Polyphemus fairy tales, it is not a giant, but a giant fish that lives in a castle. Here, the poles are stretched apart even further, and the individual elements in the tale are even more extremely isolated and united. The fairy tale frees things and people from their natural context and places them in new relationships, which can also be easily dissolved. The feeling of freedom and lightness emanating from the fairy tale has many roots. One of the strongest is the ease with which it can isolate all things, and then, just as easily, establish new relationships. In former times especially, the fairy tale could give its hearer—inseparably bound to his everyday surroundings, placed in a stable community and committed to it—at least the feeling that man, in contrast to plants and animals, is destined to dissolve his accustomed ties and enter into new ones. We often refer to our present-day world as a modern fairy tale, and this is indeed so: not only in the sense that nowadays doors open by themselves when we wish to enter a shop, that music comes forth at the touch of a button, that distant forms appear on a screen as they once did in a magic looking glass, and that we can be carried through the air faster than a thief of Bagdad ever was on his flying capret. Our world is a modern fairy tale also in a more fundamental, deeper sense: modern man has become so highly mobile, he breaks away so easily from his accustomed envirnoment, goes to faraway places and is prepared for whatever he may encounter; his existence is like that which, for centuries, only fairy-tale figures enjoyed.

Commencing with a consideration of style, we have, as if by chance, discovered the relationship of the fairy tale to life. In this regard, another motif must be mentioned which is found in our tale and in fairy tales generally. The little earth-cow forbids the girl to let her sister in the house. At once one feels reminded of the Snow White tale which we have once alluded to in a Swiss version. One also recalls that fairy tales generally have a predilection for prohibitions. Little Marie and many other fairy-tale figures are forbidden to open a certain door to enter a certain room; the bear's bride must not cast a light on him at night or she mustn't tell her parents that he can change himself into a handsome youth; Gretel is warned against telling anyone about the little earth-cow. The many prohibitions, stipulations, and precisely stated tasks are again primarily just an element of fairy-tale *style*. They help to give the fairy tale its conciseness. But underlying these severe prohibitions and commands, one senses a way of thinking similar to that in the taboos of primitive peoples. Man constructs for himself a moral world; he sets himself goals, but also limits which are set not by nature but by the human mind. The many tasks given to the fairy-tale hero offer him great opportunities, but the prohibitions place limits upon him and put him to the test. However, even when he oversteps these limits, he is not necessarily destroyed; rather, he may be led on roundabout ways through distress and sorrow to higher goals. The commands, prohibitions, and tasks in the fairy tale reflect human existence with uncanny clarity—regulated by aspirations, goals, and limitations.

In addition to this general meaning of the prohibitions, one can perhaps detect another specific significance in the plea of the beast-prince or the little earth-cow not to be betrayed. Animals play a significant and varied role in fairy tales. Two basic forms are the animal which threatens man—appearing in its most extreme form as a dragon—and the animal which brings aid, like the little earth-cow. Our tale, which shows us the nature of this helping beast from yet another aspect, continues as follows: Gretel's sister starts out one day to hunt for the little outcast in the forest. She wanders around, night comes, and now Anny, too, climbs a tree. From there she discovers the same little house and, as one might imagine, is finally let in despite the prohibition.

> And then she asked her sister in a friendly way to tell her who lived there and saw to it that she was so handsomely clothed. The good, little Gretel, who was forbidden to say to whom this house belonged, thought up many excuses. Once she said it was a wolf, the next time she said a bear. Anny believed none of this and gently coaxed her little sister in a sweet voice to tell the truth. And the little girl (who like all women, was wont to babble more than she ought to) became very talkative and said to her sister: this house belongs to a little earth-cow. But be careful not to betray me!
> When Anny—who was still not satisfied with all the treachery

she had perpetrated against her sister—heard that, she soon said, "Very well, lead me back to the right path, so that I may return home." That Gretel quickly did, and when little Anny got home she told her mother how she had found her sister living in a little earth-cow's house and how elegantly she was dressed. "Very well," said the mother, "next week we shall go and get the little earth-cow and bring it home along with Gretel, then we will slaughter the cow and eat it."

The little earth-cow knew all these things, and when it returned home late in the evening, it cried and said to the little girl, "Alas, my dearest Gretel, look what you have done—you have let your deceitful sister in and told her whose house this is. Now your mother and sister will come out next week and take us both home with them. They will slaughter and eat me, but they will keep you with them and treat you worse than ever before."

After saying this, the little earth-cow looked so sad that the poor little girl began to cry. She was sorry she had let her sister in and was so sad that she thought she would die. But the little earth-cow consoled her, saying, "Very well, now, my dear little girl, what has happened cannot be undone. Therefore, do the following: after the butcher has slaughtered me, stay there and cry; and when he asks you what you want, tell him, "I would like so much to have my earth-cow's tail." He will give it to you, and when he does, begin crying again and ask for one of my horns. When you have that, too, cry again! When you are asked again, tell him, "I would like so much to have my earth-cow's shoe." And when you have that, go away and plant the tail in the ground, the horn on top of the tail and the little shoe on top of the horn; then leave, and do not return until the third day. And on the third day it will have grown into a tree which in summer and in winter will bear the most beautiful apples anyone has ever seen. And no one will be able to pick them but you alone, and with the help of this tree you will become a great and powerful woman."

Then one day a nobleman comes riding along. The beautiful apples can bring his sick son back to health. But when the older sister and the stepmother try to pick the apples, the branches pull away, just as in the Grimm's fairy tale of One-eye, Two-eyes, and Three-eyes. Only to Gretel do the branches willingly offer themselves; she can give the apples to the youth and afterward ride away with him in the coach and become his wife.

The dragon and the little earth-cow represent the destructive and helpful, devouring and sustaining, aspects of animals which are also found in reality. Man experiences animals as friend or foe, and both have symbolic significance. When Schiller speaks of the battle with the dragon, he means ultimately the internal struggle with one's own drives and feelings. The hardest battle is the stuggle with oneself. Each man is his own worst enemy. Modern psychology believes that our own unconscious can appear to us as an animal or a dragon. It prepares to devour us, but in our battle with it, we win the princess. Only this confrontation with the demon leads us to the highest goal and makes us the king whose redemption is expressed in the image of the marriage with the beautiful maiden. The helping animal in the fairy tale can embody unconscious forces within us. The name "Little Earth-Cow" thus acquires a special sense: our feelings, bound to nature and not yet distorted by the intellect, can nourish and guide us. But not only the little earth-cow must be killed in order to bring greater redemption in a different form. Elsewhere in the fairy tale, the helping animal—the fox, wolf, or horse—instructs its protégé, in the end, to cut off its head. And when, with great reluctance, this is done, the helping animal is transformed into a radiant prince. The same thing happens to the frog which is flung against the wall. Lower natures are to be transformed into higher ones, but this does not take place without suffering and sacrifice —and cruelty. One's own instincts—no matter how much they protect and nourish us—must not be left to themselves, or indulged and pampered; they must be enchanted or disenchanted, redeemed and purified by the power of the intellect. Thus, one may view the battle with the dragon and the encounter with the helping animal as the conflict with unconscious forces within one's own self. Both times this encounter with the unconscious leads to a higher stage of development, an enlarged awareness. However, we do not believe that such interpretations capture the total significance of the fairy tale. They only make visible certain things contained in the fairy tale. The battle with the dragon is not only a symbol for the struggle with the dark side of our un-conscious, what is evil or sinister within us, it is, of course, a symbol for the struggle against evil in the world. In a well-known fairy tale, the animal prince or the animal bride breaks the spell and becomes a real human prince or princess for the sake of the hero or heroine. This tale certainly portrays much more than just the turning of one's consciousness to his own unconscious, or the union of intellect and soul. It also depicts, for example, the ambivalent relationship between man and woman. The great writer Novalis, it seems to me, has said something especially significant. He asks if such tales do not suggest "that when man overcomes himself he also overcomes nature and a miracle takes place. In one tale a bear is transformed into a prince at the moment he is loved. Perhaps a similar transformation would occur if man began to love the evil in the world." We might add that the fairy tale suggests this in images which produce a much more powerful effect on the mind and heart of its hearers than do moralistic doctrines.

CHAPTER 6

THE LIVING DOLL

Local Legend and Fairy Tale

It is 150 years now since the Grimm brothers published their fairy tales. Shortly thereafter, they published two volumes of German local legends. Both of these works were like a clarion call: all over the world people began collecting and publishing tales and legends. Since then, countless books of this kind have appeared, and scholars in the most diverse disciplines have proceeded to investigate the treasures brought to light. Ethnologists, folklorists, and religious historians viewed them as evidence of ancient beliefs and the manner in which the world was experienced; psychologists interpreted them along with dreams as an expression of unconscious processes in the mind. Literary scholars were interested in the poetic quality of fairy tales and local legends. Have such stories been awakened to a new life through all these publications? In a certain way, they have—especially for young people. But in our present era of newspapers, magazines, radio, and television, the oral tradition by which fairy tales were passed down from generation to generation has been, not only disturbed, but practically destroyed. The gap has been filled by books of tales and legends. Parents and teachers tell fairy tales to children just as they have found them in the book, or they read them aloud. The fairy tales of the Grimm brothers are still the most popular source.

The situation is somewhat different with regard to the local legend, which is bound up much more closely than the fairy tale with the personal milieu of the narrator and his hearer. For a boy reading in such books about the ghost of the Alps or a mermaid, local legends can possess a subjective reality comparable in effect to that of the fairy tales he had heard in early childhood. But what about the oral presentation of tales and legends in adult circles? We know that at one time they were both told by and for adults. The fairy tale today—like the bow and arrow, the toma-hawk, and the feathered headdress—has sunk to the level of the children's playroom. Local legends and similar stories are still told among grownups at an evening gathering, but they, too, are gradually losing their viability for external and internal reasons. The evening gathering, with its common activity and discussion, no longer has the importance it once did. In addition, the con-sequences of the Enlightenment—only now being felt in isolated areas—have undermined the local legend from within. Neverthe-less, both local legend and fairy tale have been told for centuries in Europe, passed down from one generation to the next. The two genres—like the ballad and epic, tragedy and comedy—each seem to correspond to a basic expectation or experience of man. We shall now compare an Alpine legend from the canton of Uri in Switzerland and a modern Greek fairy tale of similar theme.

The Tunsch Baptized
by the Cowherds of Göschenen

> It is said that ancient chronicles report how, many, many years ago, the mountain pasture began right behind the houses of Göschenen. At that time the hamlet of Abfrutt did not yet exist.
>
> In this pasture lived wanton servants who led a dissolute life, did not say their prayers and scoffed at sacred things and God's commandments. Once they took some odds and ends and made a

Dittitolgg, or as it is also called, a Tunsch, Tunggel, Dittitunsch or Tschungg. They played all sorts of foolish pranks with it, smeared it with cream and pudding and finally went so far as to baptize it. Now it came to life and began to talk. After they had recovered from their first shock they resumed their mischief and behaved more and more dissolutely. After some time had passed, the Toggel began to climb up on the roof of the hut at night, where it trotted about like a horse. In the autumn, when the men came down from the mountain pasture, they forgot the milking stool. But when they noticed it, nobody wanted to go back to get it, for they were afraid. So they cast lots, and the task fell to the worst one of them. He returned while the others continued with the cattle. When they got to the top of the hill where Abfrutt stands today, they looked back and saw a ghost stretching out their comrade's skin on the roof of the hut.

Since that time a dreadful ghost lived there and the pasture could no longer be used.

This is a short, simple tale. But it at once makes the nature of the local legend clear to us. A local legend is a report—sometimes quite formless and unpolished—of a weird, frightful event, and thus it is a primitive narrative form. Normal daily events need not be talked about. There is a saying: "He who takes a trip has something to tell." The teller of the legend takes a trip to a very different world, one which lies behind the mundane reality of everyday life. The germinal form of the legend is most likely the simple assertion that one has seen something uncanny at a certain time in a certain place—a woman in white or a man glowing like fire—or, perhaps has heard or felt something: the ghostly huntsmen racing through the night sky. These descriptions by themselves are brief interpretations; it was perhaps only a white cloud of mist, a gleam of light, or a whirlwind that startled the individual. When one has given form to the uncanny phenomenon, classifying and labeling it, he has taken the first step toward overcoming it. One can continue from this point: the woman in white is a poor soul in need of salvation; the fiery man has come to warn against wickedness; the ghostly chase is the army of the dead, led by Wotan. Every interpretation offers the individual reassurance to a certain degree by classifying what is intangible and mysterious, and thereby depriving it of some of its ominous power. On the other hand, the interpretation of these phenomena as belonging to the world of the dead further intensifies the feeling of horror, for the world of the dead in itself is frightening to the living. Here, too, the dual quality of all human endeavors becomes apparent. The interpretation, as such, is a defense, a self-protective mechanism, on the part of the storyteller; but the type of interpretation he provides lets the threatening and horrifying aspects of the experience reappear more strongly than before in a new way. The legend of the cowherds' Tunsch, Ditti, or Dittitolgg has been recorded in many versions, not only in the mountains of Uri, but also in the alpine regions of the cantons of Bern and Valais, and in Austria. (It is to this extent migratory and not merely local.) The ghastliness of what happens is stressed in a manner completely different from that of the fairy tale. One variant from Golzer reads:

> In a solemn and firm tone of voice, the Toggel ordered the cowherd who was the overseer of the pasture to remain. He permitted the others to leave, but warned them not to look back until they had reached the turn. Thus it happened that the cowherd remained while the others started out with the cattle; and when they had reached the turn they looked back and, trembling with horror, watched as the Toggel stretched out the cowherd's bloody skin on the roof of the hut. Ever since, the place has been called "Butcher's Mountain."

In the fairy tale, we do not see any blood flow or any wounds open up when a helping animal or someone who fails to solve a riddle is decapitated, or when an evil queen is pulled apart by four horses. Rumpelstiltskin tears himself in half right down the middle, but no one visualizes it literally: exactly equal halves result, as if a little man made of paper were cut in two. The fairy tale removes the realistic elements, whereas the local legend forces us to view events realistically. The ninety-nine heads of the unsuccessful suitors which are set up on display on top of the city wall seem almost ornamental. The very pluralization prevents us from putting ourselves in their places and sympathizing with the suffering of these unfortunate creatures. However, the hearer experiences with a shudder of horror the fate of the hapless cowherd from Golz or Göschenen in the mountain pasture. In the fairy tale, a cruel execution does not really destroy the victim's good looks: the armless girl in her symmetrical mutilation does not seem at all repulsive in our imagination. But in the local legend, the destruction of the cowherd is clearly pictured right down to the organic details. How consistent both fairy tale and local legend are in their style is shown in the fact that supernatural figures in the fairy tale are generally very well proportioned; in the local legend, they have distorted features, manifested, for example, in the Valais masks which have become so well-known. The Dittitolgg or Tunsch is a deformed and distorted figure made of bits and pieces of trash. The cowherds smear its face with rice pudding and cream and say, "Now eat it!" And when it does, it gradually swells up, according to several variants. In the local legend, the uncanny, destructive forces are at work in all directions. It is a great relief and release to turn from this genre back to the fairy tale.

Mr. Simigdáli or the Gentleman Made of Groats

> *Our fairy tale begins.*
> *Good evening,*
> *and welcome.*

Once upon a time many years ago there was a king who had a daughter, and she had many suitors. But she rejected them all, because none was pleasing to her. Thus, she contrived to make a man for herself. She took a kilogram of almonds, a kilogram of sugar and a kilogram of groats, mixed them all together, kneaded it into the shape of a man and placed it before the saint's image in her house. Then she knelt down and began to pray. Forty days and forty nights she prayed, and after the forty days God brought to life this man of groats and people called him Mr. Simigdáli or Mr. Groats. He was extremely handsome, and the whole world heard about him and knew his name. So, too, did a queen in a very dis-

tant kingdom, and she decided to go and abduct Mr. Simigdáli. She
had a golden ship built with golden oars and traveled to the city
where he lived. Then she said to her sailors, "Go ashore and seize
the one who is distinguished by his handsomeness and bring him
back to the ship to me." When the people heard of the arrival of a
golden ship, they all ran to see it, as did Mr. Simigdáli. The sailors
recognized him almost as soon as they saw him, and they seized him
and at once dragged him onto the ship.

In the evening the king's daughter waited and waited for Mr.
Simigdáli—in vain! She inquired everywhere and learned that a
queen had seized him and sailed off with him. What was to happen
now? What could she do? She had three pairs of iron shoes made
and started out on her search for Mr. Simigdáli. She went to many
lands, she left many lands, she traveled far away from the world
and finally came to the mother of the moon.—"I wish you good
fortune, mother of the moon!"—"And good luck to you, my dear
girl; how did you get to this place?"—"My good fortune brought me
here. Have you not seen Mr. Simigdáli somewhere?"—"How could
I, my dear? This is the first time I have heard his name. Sit down
until my child comes. It travels around the world and may have
seen him." When the moon came, its mother went over to it and
said, "My child, this girl here wants to know if you haven't seen Mr.
Simigdáli somewhere."—"How could I? I haven't seen him. She
really should go to the sun. It sees more of the world and may have
seen him." The moon and its mother gave the king's daughter an
almond and told her, "Whenever you are in need, break it."

Here, in the fairy tale, the creation of the puppet is the first
episode in an involved tale. From this point, the plot broadens
and begins to unfold in the manner of the fairy tale, and this alone
contributes a great deal toward making the fairy tale light, bright,
and airy. In the local legend, the plot does not move; it withdraws
into itself, so to speak, and is tied to a certain locale. Nevertheless,
there are a remarkably large number of parallels between the two
tales in the episode in which the puppet is created and brought to
life. The fairy-tale princess kneads her puppet out of groats, sugar,
and almonds; in the local legend, the cowherds' doll is usually
made of wood and rags, but there is a variant in which they form
it from a mass of cheese. The princess wishes to create a man for

herself; the cowherds have a female in mind. The cowherds baptize their creation; the Greek princess asks God to bring it to life. The princess places the puppet in front of the saint's image in her house; and in Uri, variants can be found in which the doll is placed in the corner of the room where the crucifix is. But how different the atmosphere in the fairy tale is from that in the local legend! In the fairy tale, a man is created who is handsome to the point of perfection and without a single abnormal feature; in the local legend, it is a sort of formless mass that swells up in an ominous fashion. And again we observe that a very specific basic style prevails in each of the two tales. In the fairy tale, not only the characters are perfected and clearly formed: so is the extensive, well-organized plot. The princess acts from the very outset with a clear awareness of her goal; she has the firm resolve to form a husband for herself. We are not at all speaking here in the figurative sense, but the wording unexpectedly contributes to the psychological interpretation of the fairy tale. The cowherds' intention to bring the doll to life is not nearly so distinct; they hardly have any inkling of the consequences of their wanton and sinful actions. In the fairy tale, it is clearly the work of God that the puppet is finally brought to life; in the local legend, where everything remains indistinct and mysterious, one is not sure just what uncanny forces cause the doll to come to life. The baptism and the placing of the doll in the corner of the room where the crucifix hangs are wanton blasphemy in the local legend; but in the fairy tale, the prayer and the placing of the groats and sugar man in front of the saint's image seem to be part of a meaningful activity and, hence, quite innocuous. God does not feel at all offended, but fulfills the wish of this lady who found no man in His creation suitable, and brings her puppet to life. What mysterious impulses induce the cowherds in their lonely hut to mock God? We learn nothing about this. But in the fairy tale, the motives of the characters are clearly expressed, in conformance here, too, with the over-all clarity of style. The central theme in the local legend—the animation of the doll—becomes a mere episode in the fairy tale. There is no astonishment and no alarm: the man who has just been created is joyfully greeted by all present. In some of the local legends, on the other hand, the cow-herds look at their creation come to life with a mixture of horror, insolence, and lust. There is in the local legend an intensity of feeling which is both strongly religious and erotic; in the fairy tale there is neither. The one lady calmly and resolutely asks God to fulfill a most immodest wish, and the other lady just as calmly and resolutely steals the man she wants. No emotion can be detected; everything internal has been externalized. Feelings and aspirations appear as actions or gestures, relationships as gifts. Our princess easily establishes contact with God, and just as easily and naturally, with the moon, sun, and stars, as well. Only the three pairs of iron shoes which she wears out on the way suggest that the journey is toilsome and that the princess has to suffer. Here, again, something internal is externalized and presented purely as an image. The princess received an almond from the moon and its mother; later, she receives a walnut from the sun and the sun's mother, and a hazelnut from the stars and the stars' mother.

The princess took the hazelnut and left. She traveled many different roads and finally arrived at the place where Mr. Simigdáli was kept. Disguised as a beggar, she went to the palace and saw him; but he didn't recognize her and she said nothing. She went to the servants and asked, "Won't you let me sleep with the geese?" The servants took the princess to where the geese were kept, and in the morning when she awoke, she broke the almond. Out came a golden spindle with a golden reel and a little golden wheel. The servants saw this miracle, and as fast as their legs could carry them, they ran to the queen and told her about it. The queen listened and then said to the servants, "Run to her and tell her to give the golden spindle with the golden reel and the little golden wheel to us, and ask her what she wants in return." The servants ran back to the beggar girl and asked her. "I will give you the spindle," she said. "All you need do is to bring Mr. Simigdáli here to me for one evening."—"What harm can be done in letting him spend an evening with her!" said the queen. "What can happen?"

In the evening the queen gave Mr. Simigdáli a sleeping potion, and Mr. Simigdáli had scarcely finished drinking it before he fell asleep. The servants picked him up and carried him to the beggar girl, then seized the golden spindle with the little golden wheel and left. Now the princess began to speak to Mr. Simigdáli: "Why don't you wake up? Here am I, who prepared the almonds, who kneaded and prayed; here am I, who made you, who wore through three pairs of iron shoes in order to find you. Do you not have a little sympathy for me, my dearest?" All night long she exhorted him, but how could he wake up? In the morning, the servants came and carried Mr. Simigdáli away, and the queen gave him another potion, and he woke up.

The second night passes in the same fashion; and the foreign queen gets the golden hen and its golden chicks, which emerged from the walnut. The hazelnut, finally, contains a bush of golden carnations; and now, the third time, comes the turn of events.

Nearby the goose house there lived a tailor, and all night long he heard the conversation. He took Mr. Simigdáli aside and said to him, "Your Majesty, may I ask you a question? Where do you sleep at night?"—"In my house, where else? And why do you ask?"—"Mr. Simigdáli, for the last two evenings as I closed my eyes to go to sleep I have heard the beggar girl in the goose house who talks all night, saying, 'Mr. Simigdáli, why don't you wake up? I have worn my shoes out in order to find you, and you don't speak to me!'" And Mr. Simigdáli understood. He went to his horse and got it ready, and in the evening, when the queen again tried to give him the sleeping potion, he did not drink, but pretended he had fallen asleep. The servants picked him up and carried him to the beggar girl, and took the carnation bush away with them. When the princess again began to pour out her grief, Mr. Simigdáli arose, embraced her, and at once they mounted the horse and left.

In the morning they went to get Mr. Simigdáli again—but where was he? When the queen learned that Mr. Simigádli had disappeared, she began to cry—but what could she do? She spoke, "I, too, will make myself a man!" She ordered the servants to crack open some almonds and mix them with sugar and groats, and from this she kneaded a man. She knelt before him, but instead of praying she uttered curses, and after forty days the man had rotted and was thrown away.

The princess returned to her kingdom with Mr. Simigdáli and they lived more and more happily ever after.

Thus, the fairy tale here, at the conclusion, returns with artistic effect to the beginning. It sketches a sort of little anti-fairy tale. The heroine who has found favor with God is contrasted with the anti-heroine who has not. Her curses correspond to the cowherds' wanton behavior. Good and evil, pious and sinful qualities are carefully allotted to various characters. Everything complex in reality is simplified in the fairy tale. One thinks of the remark made by Hugo von Hofmannsthal on viewing an open landscape freely unfolding before us: "In our body the whole universe is crushed together; how blissful it is to relieve oneself of this dreadful burden." But what shall we make of the motif of the groats-and-sugar man? It does not often appear in fairy tales throughout the world. But it so happens that we know of several versions from Greece and Italy. In most of them, sugar is the crucial ingredient, and this gives us a clue. Viewed psychologically, our Greek princess creates her own lover. She does not love another human being, she loves an image that she has made for herself and which she now cares for and caresses. She does not love another, she loves herself. The image which she has in her mind is sweet, and she gives herself up to it the way Hansel and Gretel do to the sugar in the gingerbread house. Psychologically speaking, she makes herself an ideal image which she transfers to a person. She does not really love the other person, she loves the sweet image which originated within her. But the fairy tale tears away from her this person she has made, and the princess who only wanted sugar, groats, and almonds now has to run around until she has worn out three pairs of iron shoes. She has to experience suffering and privation, and not until her creation has been alienated from her can she regain it. The man of sugar has now become an individual, and she loves him now for his sake and no longer just for her own. From this point, the final turn of events seems like a repetition of the first part of the tale. Again a princess tries to fashion a man for herself out of marzipan, but this time the puppet rots. The second princess is only another form of the first one: her primitive, childish, sugar-addicted component, from which she now breaks away and enters a new stage of development, where she lives "more and more happily ever after." The gloomy local legend, however, shows how man can fall victim to his own creation and be destroyed by it.

The contrast with the local legend has revealed the superior ease with which the fairy tale handles its motifs. It sublimates reality. It empties the motifs and removes them from reality. This is, however, not only a loss, but a gain: they become transparent and weightless. The fairy tale is, to use a phrase coined by Hermann Hesse, a "playing with glass beads." Things which are, in reality, weighty and difficult become light and transparent. Not only do feelings become light and volatile; not only do crime and justice playfully take their places in this stylized world; the erotic, the divine, the magical are also not present in their original form and power. When a fairy-tale hero receives a hair from a wolf, he need only rub it, and the wolf—who once received kindness from him—hastens to his aid. Again, a relationship, this time between a person and a helping animal, is concretized in something manifest. When the hero rubs the hair, we do not feel the exertion of the magician's will power. Nor do we imagine that the wolf, whose hair, *pars pro toto*, is being rubbed between the hero's fingers, is suffering great pain and is forced through the power of such magic to come running. The rubbing of the hair is only a signal; the wolf comes running of his own free will. All magic which appears in the fairy tale is light and effortless. Therefore, one should not speak of magic in the strict sense. The magical in the fairy tale is sublimated, as is everything profane, erotic, and religious. This sublimation of all its elements makes it possible for the fairy tale to encompass the world in all its essential parts in an altered form. This world and the hereafter, sun and stars, city and countryside, forest and sea, king and swineherd, princess and Cinderella, love and envy and betrayal, weddings, murder, death sentences, battles, power, splendor, poverty, magic spells, suffering, curse, and redemption: the whole world is reflected in the glass pearls of the fairy tale. In another variant of the Greek fairy tale here discussed, the heroine lures her rival with three golden dresses: "One was the heavens with its stars, the second was the earth with its flowers, and the third the sea with the golden fish." And in another Greek fairy tale, a fig, a nut, and a hazelnut each contain a dress. On one "the month of May could be seen with its flowers"; on the second "the heavens could be seen with its stars"; and on the third "the sea could be seen with its waves." One cannot express more beautifully how the world is woven into the clothing of man in the fairy tale, how the enormous patterns of the cosmos are connected with man in a manageable and beneficial form, and how man is securely established in the realm of heaven and earth, and assimilates them both. The flowers, stars, and waves in man's garment are only a reflection of the real waves and stars; but the mere fact that man is able to capture the earth and cosmos in such a reflection and establish connection with them brings his redemption. Only the sublimating, volatile style makes it possible for the fairy tale to assimilate the elements of the world and, having arranged them in beautiful order through the context of the tale, to make them understood and appreciated by the hearer. Thus, the fairy tale includes the hearer in this order, sheltering him in it as only a true work of art can do.

CHAPTER 7

ANIMAL STORIES

A Glimpse of the Tales
of Primitive Peoples

When we compare European fairy tales with those of non-European origin, two things can be clearly established from the outset. The tales of the civilized Oriental peoples known to us in the *Thousand and One Nights* and other collections are, for the most part, carefully and artfully fashioned literary works. They may be based in part on folk tales, but we have no knowledge of what the latter might have been like. And among primitive peoples, like the African Negroes and American Indians, fairy tales in the strict sense are practically nonexistent. With European tales, we can fairly well distinguish between local legends, saints' legends, fairy tales, fables, and realistic jests; with primitive peoples, however, such specialization simply does not occur. Specialization in each form has been highly cultivated in Europe. It is a characteristic of primitive tales that everything is still rolled up all together, undifferentiated and undeveloped, as in the seed of a plant, and that the unfolding and structuring are left to a later stage of development. Neither among the primitive peoples nor among the civilized peoples of the Near and Far East, for example, has the theater unfolded and developed into such strictly differentiated genres as it has in Europe, where we have, side by side, drama, opera, and ballet. Among primitive peoples, and to a large extent as well among the Orientals, dance, song, instrumental music, and dialogue are all combined in one. And, like the European theater, European narrative literature is also characterized by a tendency to unfold and separate into various genres.

Among the primitives, animal stories predominate. They are part myth, part fable, part fairy tale. Primitive peoples live in close contact with wild animals: they hunt them, but they also fear them, even revere them, and believe in their power. In tales of the American Indians, the heroes are animals and stars, not human beings, as in the European fairy tale. In these tales, animals are creator and ruler of the world. They are also the bearers of culture: man must use trickery to get water from the water snake; he gets fire from the frog; and he could not even invent sleep by himself, he learned it by watching the sleepy lizard. Here, it is hard to determine where the boundary lies between myths that were believed and impertinent jesting. However, it has been established that some primitive peoples and even East Indian storytellers firmly believe that people at times are transformed into animals or even can transform themselves into such. Much that we feel to be symbolic in our fairy tales is accepted by primitive peoples as unvarnished fact, so that here one can scarcely speak of fairy tales in the strict sense. Even the journey to the underworld is believed to be within the capabilities of the magician or shaman; he undertakes it in order to get a magic cure for a sick man or even to bring back someone who has died. Magical power is ascribed to the tales themselves. Just as the Indians, with their feathered headdresses, hope to acquire the powers of the birds from which the feathers are taken, they also hope, by telling of the deeds of animals, to attract some of the animals' power to themselves. The Asiatic Koryaks tell how the giant raven flies up to heaven in order to put an end to the incessant rain. This story may only be told while it is raining, never in good weather, for it is a charm against rain. Here, we believe we are close to the origins of the fairy tale. Waking dreams, delirium, ecstasy, shamanic rapture, belief in magic and magic rites, are some of the roots of the fairy tale. The fairy tale itself, with its lightheartedness is an advanced form of all these elements.

As we have previously indicated, the animal story can assume playful forms among primitive peoples as well; stories similar in nature to the local legend and myth are joined by those similar in fables. The tale of the race between two animals is known and loved the world over. Here is an American Indian version:

The Race between the Flea and the Ostrich

> The flea and the ostrich wanted to hold a race to see who was the best runner. At the start of the race, the flea hopped up into a corner of the ostrich's eye and held on tight.
>
> When the ostrich had run some distance it glanced to the side to see if the flea was there too. Since it was sitting in the corner of the eye, the ostrich saw it at its side.
>
> The ostrich ran faster and when it had gone a little way looked to the side again and saw that the flea was still there.
>
> The ostrich ran as fast as it could. When it was very close to the finish, the flea jumped out of the corner of its eye and was the first to arrive. The flea had won the race.

The realism in this tale is especially charming. Unlike the European tale, in which the hare does not see the hedgehog until they arrive at their goal, the flea, by virtue of an optical illusion, appears constantly at the ostrich's side. (The flea in question is one of those grey bloodsuckers which also like to attach themselves to our dogs at eye level.) But, of course, the skillful combination of realism and fantasy is not all there is to this Indian story. It has, at the same time, a symbolic significance. All these stories about races belong to the large group of tales in which a large or strong animal is outwitted by a small, insignificant, or weak one. It is the consolation of the slave, who can defend himself only by cunning from his master, whether the latter be a tribal chieftain or a white plantation owner. Such tales are as popular among African tribes as among North American Negroes

and South American Indians. They clearly have social implications, but one must immediately add that this does not exhaust
the interpretation. The vision of the victory of the humble over
the mighty, the stories of David and Goliath, of the clever dwarf
and the dumb giant, derive from the knowledge or supposition
of, or belief in the power of, the humble, the obscure, and the
minute. The intelligence of frail man overcomes the giants of
nature, the invisible, atom-sized particle contains incredible
power. Thus, a tale must usually be interpreted on several planes,
even when it is as short and simple as the South American Indian
tale of the flea and the ostrich. When we speak of the flea and the
ostrich, or of David and Goliath, we at first automatically identify
with the victor—David or the flea. But both stories can also be
seen in a different light. The humble conquers the mighty. The
ostrich can suddenly become the symbol for man, who runs and
runs and anxiously looks to the side and cannot understand and
finally sees himself conquered by a scarcely visible but treacher-
ous opponent. And as soon as the tale appears to us in this light,
we can no longer comprehend how we originally identified with
the flea rather than with the helpless, so much more human, ostrich. The humorous animal tale has become a tormenting vision.
Some of these stories about races end with the killing of the larger
animal. Such is the case in the race between the horsefly and the
fox, as told by the Araucanians in Chile.

The Race between the Horsefly and the Fox

"Let's play a game, my friend!" said the fox to the horsefly. "Fine,"
the horsefly answered, "what shall we play?" "Let's have a race,"
said the fox. "You run along the ground and I will run above the
ground." "Fine," the horsefly replied. "Let's make that oak tree
over there our goal," the fox said. "Fine," answered the horsefly.

So they had a race. But just as the fox was about to run off, the
horsefly sat down on the fox's tail.

So the fox ran away.

And as he was running along as fast as he could he caught
sight of some strawberries. "I will sit down here for a moment and
eat some strawberries," the fox said. "I just wonder where the ras-

cally horsefly is?" Then the fox set about eating the strawberries. "After all, I'll get to the goal in a short while," he said. Now when he had almost arrived, the horsefly quickly hopped down and ran for the goal, and thus became the winner.

"Pay me my winnings!" the horsefly demanded. "I don't care to," said the fox. "Be happy I don't eat you up!" Then the horsefly called together its comrades. One hundred came, two hundred, five hundred, six hundred. From all sides they crawled into the fox and stung him inside the belly. He leaped into the water but the horse-flies continued to sting him. Then he ran toward the forest and at the edge of the forest they killed him.

Thus, the clever fox, who as a rule appears as a crafty fellow in Indian and other tales, falls victim to the tiny grey insect. Another South American story tells how the tortoise kills the jaguar. The tortoise's little son cries because he wants to have the jaguar's claws to play with. Now the jaguar was actually about to eat the tortoise, but the sly tortoise coaxes it to the point of killing itself. How does the tortoise accomplish this? It climbs up a tall, thorny tree and then lets itself roll down, without suffering any injury. The jaguar is amused by this and twice makes the tortoise show him how it was done. "The jaguar wanted to attempt this, too," it states at the end of the short tale. "It climbed up and rolled down, but tore open all its entrails on the thorns and died." Thus the insidious tortoise brings about the downfall of the stately jaguar; it entices the jaguar to destroy itself, and now the tortoise's child can play with the jaguar's claws. It is not only the presentiment of social judgment in our own times which makes us feel the gloomy side of such tales. South American Indians themselves are filled with the sorrow of such feelings and many of their tales are melancholy or bitter. That can also be said of some African tales. As an example, we shall take a longer story with a whole series of episodes in which animals are no longer actually in the foreground, a tale of the East African Bantus.

The Fairy Tale of Mrile

A man had in the course of time three sons. Now the oldest went off with his mother to dig up Kolokasia tubers. In doing this he found a tuber that had gone to seed, and said, "Oh, here is a tuber as good looking as my little brother!" But his mother said to him, "How can a tuber be as good looking as a human child?" But he hid the tuber while his mother was tying the Kolokasias together to carry them home. He hid it in the hollow of a tree and then he said to it, *"msura kwivire-vire tsa kambingu na kasanga."* The next day he went back to it. Now the tuber had become a child. His mother cooked the food and he carried it away. Every day he carried the food to the hollow in the tree while he himself grew thinner and thinner. His father and mother saw how he was losing weight and asked, "Son, what is making you so thin? What happens to the food we always cook for you? After all, your younger brothers haven't become so thin." One day his younger brothers watched while the food was prepared and he received his portion. He didn't eat, however, but carried the food away as if he were going to save it. His brothers followed him at a distance and watched what he did. They saw him putting the food in the hollow of the tree, and when they returned home told his mother, "We saw him take the food to the hollow of a tree and give it to a child there." She answered them, "What child does one find in a tree?" But they said to her, "Very well, we will show you the way there, mother." And they led her there and showed her the place. And lo and behold—there in the hollow of the tree was a little child! And the mother beat the child and killed it. After she had killed the little child, Mrile took food to it, but found it had been killed. He returned home and wept with all his heart. Then they asked, "Mrile, why are you crying?" But he answered, "It is just the smoke in my eyes." They said to him, "Sit over here on the lower side." But he continued to cry. And they said to him, "Why do you continue to cry?" And he answered, "It is nothing but the smoke." Thereupon they said, "Take your father's chair and go out and sit in the yard." He took the chair, sat down in the yard, and continued to weep. Then he said, "Chair, reach up into the sky like the rope on which my father hangs the honey pot in the jungle and on the steppes." And the chair rose up into the sky and became caught on a tree. Again he said, "Chair, reach up into the sky like the rope on which my father hangs the honey pot in the jungle and on the steppes." Just then, his younger brothers stepped into the yard, and they saw how he rose up into the sky. They announced to his mother, "Mrile has gone up to heaven." But she said, "Why do you tell me that your oldest brother has gone to heaven? Is there any way for him to rise up there?" They only said to her, "Come and see, mother!" And then the mother came and found he had risen up.

Then his mother called:

> "Mrile, come back,
> come back, my child,
> come back!"

But Mrile answered:

> "I shall never return,
> I shall never return,
> Mother, I say,
> I shall never return,
> I shall never return."

Then his younger brothers called out:

> "Mrile, come back,
> come back, our brother
> come back!
> come home,
> come home!"

But he said:

> "I say,
> I shall never return,
> I shall never return,
> my brothers,
> I shall never return,
> I shall never return."

Then his father came and said:

"Mrile, here is your food,
   here is your food!
Mrile, here it is!
Mrile, here is your food,
   here is your food!"

But he answered and said:

"Never again,
never again,
my father, I say,
never again,
never again."

Then his relatives came, and sang:

"Mrile, come home!
   come home!
Mrile, come!
   come home!
   come home!
Mrile, come!"

Then his uncle came, and sang:

"Mrile, come home,
   come home!
Mrile, come!
   come home,
   come home!"

But he sang, in answer:

"I say
I shall never return,
I shall never return,
uncle, I say
I shall never return,
I shall never return!"

And he vanished, so that they no longer could see him. Now
he met some wood gatherers and he greeted them, saying, "Wood

gatherers, good day! Please show me the way to the moon king."
But they said to him, "First gather some wood and then we will
show you the way there." And he broke up firewood for them. Now
they told him, "Just keep on going and you will meet some grass
cutters!"

Mrile helps the grass cutters cut grass; then he comes to the
farmers and helps them farm; next, he comes to the cowherds, the
bean harvesters, the millet reapers, the banana-stalk searchers, the
water fetchers. He helps them all in their work, and they all
direct him a little further on his way to the moon king. In the
land of the moon king, food is eaten uncooked, since fire is unknown. But Mrile shows the people how to strike a fire and to
cook meat and roast bananas: both taste much better that way.
The moon king commands his people to purchase the fire from
Mrile with their cattle and goats. Thus, Mrile acquires a herd.
And now he decides to return home.

They let him leave with his cattle, and thus he departed. But
along the way he became tired. Now he had a bull, and the bull
spoke to him, saying, "What harm will it do me if I give you a ride
when you are so tired? If I take you on my back, will you eat me up
when I am slaughtered?" He answered, "No, I will not eat you." He
then got up on the bull's back, and the bull carried him. And he
rode along singing:

"I lack no worldly goods
The beast are mine, hurrah!
I lack no worldly goods
The cattle are mine, hurrah!
I lack no worldly goods
The livestock is mine, hurrah!
I lack no worldly goods
Mrile is coming, hurrah!
I lack no worldly goods."

And thus he returned home. When he arrived, his mother and
father rubbed him with fat. And he said to them, "You must feed
this bull until it is old, and even when it is old I will not eat its
meat." When the bull was old the father slaughtered it, and the

mother said, "Shall this bull which made my son so much work, be
eaten up without his having any?" And she hid the fat in the honey
pot. When she knew that the meat was all gone she ground some
flour, took the fat and added it to the flour. Then she took it to her
son and Mrile ate it. And when he tasted it in his mouth, the meat
spoke with him, saying, "You dare to eat me, the one who took you
on my back, despite your promise?" And added, "Be consumed,
therefore, even as you consume me!"

Then Mrile sang:

"My mother, didn't I tell you
   Not to give me the meat from the bull!"

When he tasted it a second time, his foot sank into the
ground.

But he sang:

"My mother, didn't I tell you
   Not to give me the meat from the bull!"

Thereupon he ate up all the flour. Suddenly he sank into the
ground—and that is the end of our tale.

This tale, like the local legend from Uri about the cowherd's
Tunsch and the modern Greek fairy tale about the man of groats,
concerns the animation of a doll. But the atmosphere here is
neither that of the local legend nor of the fairy tale. The mere
fact that the doll is not a figure made of rags or kneaded out of
dough, but a root, a bit of nature, changes the mood. Not wan-
tonness, as in the case of the cowherds, nor self-love, as in the case
of the princess, are at work here. A bright-eyed youth discovers in
the tuber which God has created the divine gift for higher development. He speaks a magic formula, puts aside his own food for
it, and the shoot comes to life and thrives. Mrile's ungifted
brothers betray his actions, and the mother, fearful for his life
and health, destroys the plant which has become human. Mrile's
relatives are more dull-witted and narrow-minded than he. But
they cannot save him. The capacity for higher development seems

to pass to him from the dead plant-child, and he rises up on his father's chair for the trip to the moon. The other world that he now enters presents him with gifts, but that is not all: the action is reciprocal. Mrile turns out to be a bearer of culture. While still on his journey, he takes part in cultivating activities, and in the moon kingdom he is the giver of fire, as if he were conveying the light of awareness to a yet barely conscious world. Thus, in two or three respects, Mrile reminds us of Prometheus: as a creator of man, as a bringer of fire and culture, and, lastly, in his tragic fate. But again, what a difference in atmosphere! No Promethean self-assurance inspires the boy; from the outset he is a tender, child-like awakener of the higher life, overshadowed by grief. In the end, not the decree of an Olympian god makes him sink into the earth, but a fate which unhaltingly and inexorably comes to pass. Everything is more subdued and melancholy, more unconscious than with the ancient Greeks, but for just this reason it is especially touching and convincing in its own way. The journey to heaven, which is often found in the tales of primitive peoples, reminds us of the fairy tale, as does the help rendered by the bull. But everything is more realistic, more like the local legend; the myth, the fairy tale and the local legend seem to be united in this tale. When we designate it as a culture-bringer myth and stress the toil and sorrow of the culture-bringer, his conflict with the environment and his ultimate doom, we are viewing the tale as a portrayal of an ancient event in human history. Processes of development which eternally recur or are realized at the outset become, by the nature of the myth, a clearly defined event. But the entire thing can also be viewed as a symbolic expression of an internal process, a series of events in the soul of one person. The child which grew from the tuber would then be the symbol of Mrile's new and growing independent life, which is snuffed out by the superior force of the mother. The masculine force, however—his father's chair and rope—lead him onward and upward. Mrile's journey to the moon country then becomes a journey into his own unconscious, with whose nourishing powers he makes contact and in whose constructive work he takes part. He tills the field and receives cattle. For his part, he brings the light of aware-

ness to the unconscious. The two spheres permeate one another:
consciousness illuminates the darkness of unconsciousness, and
the unconscious nourishes and supports the conscious. Yet the
meeting of the two realms involves danger; the relationship does
not always remain untroubled. Man, led astray, consumes the
powers which flow toward him from the animal sphere, and he
sinks into the ground and perishes. The fairy tale portrays very
nicely how Mrile, even after his long journey, is not the victor
once and for all. He can be misled, either by other people (specifically his mother) or, if we interpret subjectively, by a re-
actionary impulse in his own soul which is not yet the equal of his
own insight. It is also a nice touch that the trip to the land of the
moon, the land of the semiconscious, is depicted not as a *descent*
but as an *ascent*. That which is *below* is at the same time *above;*
the bull is a servant of Mrile's, and at the same time his master; it
is his bearer and destroyer. "Sink down—I could also say arise!"
says Mephisto to Faust, when he is to visit the realm of the
mothers. The psychologist sees portrayed in the fairy tale of Mrile
the destruction of man's vital power by an overattachment to the
mother. The marvelous succession of images cannot, however, be
rationalized in a single sentence; cannot be simply translated
into the language of reason. But every hearer and reader senses
that the tale concerns growth and danger, development and the
desire for development, creative and destructive actions, sacrifice,
sorrow, loss, divine grace and endowment, wealth, fortune, rising
and sinking and destruction. But all these things flow and mix
together in an unclear fashion and are neither so strictly arranged
nor so goal-directed as in the European fairy tale. This may
reflect the more childlike, unconscious, and passive existence of
primitive people as well as, perhaps, the weariness of a declining
or threatened people. It is not accidental nor is it mere snobbish
fashion today that African art exercises a significant influence on
European art. The twentieth century again feels the presence of
demonic spirits and the risk of destruction. But it finds in African
art, music, and literature not only a demonic spirit and mood of
doom but also rhythmic and vital power. Our fairy tale of Mrile
also fascinates us because of its intensity and structure, its calm

and insistent repetition of crucial phrases, and the reflection of one series of events in the other. Despite all this, the story of Mrile is anything but monotonous. We said previously that the dramatic and narrative literatures have developed into various genres to a lesser extent among primitive peoples and Orientals than with Europeans. Here, too, in the fairy tale of Mrile, we find a tale which is at the same time a drama. The verses are sung and the farewell scene, in which everyone crowds into the yard and attempts to dissuade Mrile from his ascent to heaven, one can imagine as a dramatic, or perhaps even a dance, presentation. In one part of the tale not reproduced here, there is even a sort of humorous sketch in the form of a dialogue with birds. Thus, our fairy tale of Mrile may be designated as a little, all-around work of art. It is, however, not a pure fairy tale, and one will have difficulty in finding any pure fairy tales at all among primitive peoples.

CHAPTER 8

RAPUNZEL

The Fairy Tale
as Representation
of a Maturation Process

The story of Rapunzel is familiar to us from the Grimm brothers'
collection. In the first edition of this famous book, Jacob, the
elder of the two brothers, tells the story in a short and concise
form.

> There was once a man and wife who had wished for a child
> for a long time and never got one. But finally one day the wife
> conceived a child. In the back of their house these people had a
> little window and through it they could look into a fairy's garden
> full of all kinds of plants and flowers—but no one dared to enter it.
> One day the wife stood at this window looking down into the gar-
> den when she caught sight of a very beautiful bed of rampion
> (Rapunzel). She knew that she couldn't have any of it, but began
> to desire it so much that she became very thin and wretched. Her
> husband finally became alarmed and asked the reason for her be-
> havior. "Alas, if I don't get to eat some of the rampion from the
> garden behind our house, I will surely die." The man, who loved
> his wife very much, resolved to get her some, no matter what it cost.
> Thus, one evening he climbed over the high wall, pulled up a hand-
> ful of rampion as fast as he could and brought it to his wife. She at

once took it, made herself a salad and hungrily ate it all up. But it had tasted so very, very good to her that her hunger increased threefold the next day. The man saw that he would have no peace, so he climbed down into the garden again. But he was greatly startled this time to find the fairy there who scolded him harshly for daring to enter her garden and steal from it. He excused himself as best he could with the pregnancy of his wife, saying how dangerous it was to deny her anything in that condition. Finally the fairy replied, "Well, then, I suppose I shall let you take as much rampion as you want; but in return you must give me the child that you wife is now carrying." In his fright the man agreed to everything, and when the woman gave birth the fairy appeared at once, called the girl Rapunzel and took the child away with her.

Rapunzel now became the most beautiful child under the sun, but when she was twelve years old the fairy took her and locked her in a tall, tall tower which had neither door nor staircase but only a tiny window way up near the top. Now when the fairy wanted to get in she stood below and called,

> "Rapunzel, Rapunzel!
> Let thy hair down."

Rapunzel had very beautiful hair as fine as spun gold, and when the fairy called out these words she untied it, wrapped it around a hook on the window and then the hair fell down twenty yards all the way to the bottom, and the fairy climbed up on it.

Now one day a young prince was passing through the forest in which the tower stood and saw the beautiful Rapunzel standing in her window and singing. She sang with such a sweet voice that he fell completely in love with her. But since there was no door in the tower and no ladder could reach that high he became very despondent. Nevertheless he went to the forest every day until one time he saw the fairy come and speak,

> "Rapunzel, Rapunzel!
> Let thy hair down."

And now he saw the ladder with which one could enter the tower. He remembered carefully the words one had to speak and the next day when it was dark went to the tower and called up,

> "Rapunzel, Rapunzel,
> Let thy hair down!"

> Then she untied her hair, and when it came down he tied himself on and was pulled up.

One can imagine what follows. When the fairy learns of Rapunzel's meetings with the prince, she cuts off Rapunzel's beautiful hair as punishment and banishes her to a desert. She lures the prince to the tower again with Rapunzel's golden hair, and when he sees how he has been deceived, he leaps from the window in desperation and, in his fall, loses both eyes. Now he wanders around blindly and, after years have passed, comes to the very same desert where Rapunzel ekes out an existence with the two children she has given birth to in the meantime. She recognizes him, "two of her tears fall in his eyes and they become as clear as they once were." So Jacob Grimm concludes the tale with this sentence. In the later editions Wilhelm Grimm changed, added, and embellished upon much in the fairy tale, not always for the better. In one respect, however, he improves upon his brother's tale. The mistress of the garden and the tower he no longer calls by the good name "fairy"; he calls her "a sorceress"; we can safely say "a witch." Our fairy tale does not come originally from Germany. Its home is in the Mediterranean countries, and there the old woman clearly has the characteristics of a witch. In Greece, she is called *"Drakena,"* and shows the distinctive characteristic of fairy-tale witches: she is a cannibal. The general significance of our fairy tale becomes clearer when we compare the Mediterranean parallels with the Grimm version. The basic scheme manifest behind them is something like this: a woman who desires some salad or vegetable has to promise her unborn child to a witch, whose garden the woman has entered to steal the desired plant. It is usually stipulated that the old woman shall get the child after ten, twelve or fourteen years. The important episode which now takes place is told in the following way in a version from Malta.

> Thus the girl grew up. Once, on her way to school, an old woman came up and spoke to her. The girl had never before seen the strange old woman and therefore answered somewhat curtly.

But the old woman presented her request, saying, "Child, tell your mother to bring me what she has promised!" The girl forgot these words, and the old woman, who often met her, reminded her of it again and again. Finally, she bit the girl on the arm with the only tooth she still had and cried, "This is so you don't always forget my orders." The little girl ran home and tearfully told her mother about the wicked old woman. The mother bandaged her little daughter's arm and consoled her. The little girl asked, "Mother, what shall I say if she asks me again? Will you give her what you promised?"—"Oh, tell her to take it where she finds it." The girl delivered this answer, and the old woman led her far, far away.

In another variant from Malta, the old woman bites off the child's finger and an ear lobe when the child does not deliver the message. Then, when the child brings the mother's answer—that she take for herself what was promised when she found it—the witch seizes the girl by her beautiful hair, which (so it says in the Maltese version) "was so long that it trailed along the ground, and the witch dragged her away with her as one leads away a lamb." Now the girl is taken to the tower, and there she learns all kinds of magic behind the witch's back or even under her guidance. Later, a handsome youth climbs up into the tower on the maiden's hair, and the two decide to flee. The witch pursues them, but the girl's magic leads her astray or renders her harmless. This basic scheme shows much clearer than does the Grimm tale that, viewed psychologically, the Rapunzel fairy tale is concerned with the portrayal of a process of development. The development takes place in several stages, and each transition involves danger, privation, and fear. But the dangers are overcome, and the development leads to the light. The pregnant mother's desire at the very outset is a sign of longing for a mysterious higher value; the desired plant grows only in the sorceress's garden, and it is dangerous to pick it. At the same time, human weakness is expressed in the behavior of the woman or her husband: the unborn child is abandoned to a sinister stranger; the parents are only half conscious of their responsibility. And now fate takes its course. On its way to school the child is forcibly torn from the protection of the home. A dreadful apparition carries the child off, and the painful bite stresses the terror of the transition. Psychologists have observed that nightmares involving evil spirits that come to carry off the dreamer often occur during important transitions, i.e., from infant to schoolchild, from schoolchild to young person, and also upon entering marriage or before the birth of the first child. Only with difficulty does one take leave of his old, familiar form of existence; he tends to cling desperately to what he has. He feels that every step forward involves a dying. Every process of development and maturation demands great bravery; to let go, to take leave, requires courage; fear and anxiety can occur. Primitive tribes therefore have set up their own rites of passage to protect people from the lurking demons. In our wedding customs, we can still see remnants of such protective rites. Then, when the transition has been safely made, new things can unfold. In the Maltese fairy tale—in which the child is named not Rapunzel, but Fenchelchen (fennel)—immediately after the witch bites off the child's finger and an ear lobe and drags her away by her long hair, it states : "They came to a tall tower with no steps leading to the top. And now our Fenchelchen spent a number of years in this tower, and the witch became quite fond of her and taught her many magic tricks." And in the other Maltese tale, it says, "Our Petersilchen (parsley) soon felt quite at home and after a short while no longer thought of her mother at all—so wonderful was life here." Thus, the old is cast off and the new, which at first appeared so terrifying to us, becomes familiar, develops new capabilities and powers within us, and makes life meaningful. Later, too, when the prince appears, Rapunzel (or whatever the girl is called in the particular tale) takes fright, and yet afterwards she gladly lets him abduct her. Again something new begins, again the old must be overcome and left behind: the witch is deceived or defeated, or in some cases even placated and won over by the lovers. This, then, is the structure of the Rapunzel fairy tale: it is a progression with clearly marked transitions, and the development is toward an ever fuller and richer existence, symbolized at the end in the union of youth and maiden. But what, one may ask, does a child learn from being told such fairy tales? Should one really fill their minds with stories about witches? Yes, indeed,

one *must*. The witches, devils, and villains of the fairy tale are for
children symbols of evil, and the child experiences through them
the danger of evil but also learns that evil can be conquered or
perhaps even transformed. A good illustration of the child's real
and legitimate need for a confrontation with dangerous forces in
the realm of imagination is offered by the behavior of a two-and-
one-half-year-old girl who had been told about the meeting of
Little Red Riding Hood and the wolf in the forest but not about
the further developments in the fairy tale. A little picture that
the girl got in a store showed the wolf in the grandmother's bed;
the child asked what that meant and so learned the whole story.
The next few nights she was restless and on awakening spoke
about the wolf. Everyone tried to relieve the child's fears, the
wolf's picture was cut out and burned, and she was told that there
are no more wolves today, or, if so, they are far, far away in
Russia. The child calmed down. A few weeks later the father was
going to take the child for a walk in the woods, and the mother
was carefully preparing her for it. "Now you are going to the
woods with papa to see the little bunny rabbit." The little girl
left beaming. As they came downstairs, an elderly resident met
the two hikers and asked the child where they were going. To the
father's great astonishment, she answered quietly and resolutely,
"To the woods to see the Ussian wolf." This incident, reported by
the psychologist Josephine Bilz, makes it clear that even small
children possess the readiness and, thus, no doubt the strength, to
encounter what is dangerous and frightening. Hand in hand with
her father, the child does not want to go to see the harmless
bunny rabbit, but the *wolf*. It would be wrong to purge our fairy
tales of all cruelty and all frightening characters for the sake of
children. All these things are not, after all, portrayed realistically
in the fairy tale, but figuratively, and thus the evil figures are not
perceived as living people but as symbols of evil. Hansel and
Gretel, in conquering the witch, not only overcome a wicked old
woman but evil itself. And when Rapunzel, Petersilchen, or
Fenchelchen forget their mothers in the tower, that is also not
realistically perceived as a lack of love or loyalty but as an expression of a necessary internal disengagement.

One feels that fairy tales are concerned with portraying essential processes in life. Testing, threatening danger, destruction—and salvation, development, and maturation—are portrayed before our mind's eye in images which are unreal, but for just that reason fascinating. And since the European fairy tale repeatedly portrays developments leading to a rich, regal existence, it is not only full of light and serenity, but merry and rollicking *humor* also finds a place in it. Just as the devil in the folk legend often is made to appear as an outwitted, stupid fellow and can become a comical figure, a clown in the folk plays, the witch in the fairy tale is a figure that can easily appear in a comic light. In "Hansel and Gretel," she lives in a gingerbread house and lets herself be duped by Gretel. She herself crawls into the oven, where she is burned up: a playful and by no means frightful image for the self-destruction of evil.

The Mediterranean versions of our Rapunzel fairy tale are full of smiles and droll humor. In Italian tales, even the introductory scene is imbued with such humor. Here, the wife longs for parsley and sneaks into the witch's garden at night to steal this plant.

> The witch didn't know who the thief was; therefore she wanted to catch her in the very act. She hid under the ground close by the largest bed of parsley but let one ear protrude in order to hear better. Now when the woman came to steal the parsley she saw the witch's ear and thought it was a mushroom. "Oh, what a beautiful mushroom!" she said, reaching for it as if she were going to pluck it. At that the witch, gnashing her teeth, leaped up and shouted, "Ahhh! Now I really ought to eat you up! But for the sake of the innocent soul in your body I will forgive you. Let us make a pact. If you give birth to a boy, the child shall be yours; but if it is a girl, you must give it to me."

In many fairy tales, the events in the tower are filled with humor. The Maltese Fenchelchen, whom we have already met, is visiting with her handsome young man when the old sorceress suddenly returns home.

Fenchelchen quickly transformed the youth into a footstool. A
while later the old woman said, "Please give me that stool to sup-
port my tired feet!"—"Grandmother, there are so many stools here;
take another one."—"No, that one is certainly just right for me."
The old woman now put her feet on the stool and laughed—for she
probably knew through some magic who was concealed in the form
of the stool. She remained in the tower for several days now and
had no desire to take a walk. Finally she went out; and when she
returned to the tower and called up to Fenchelchen, the girl
quickly transformed the youth into a sewing needle.

A little while later the old woman said, "Please hand me that
needle; I would like to pick my teeth with it."—"Grandmother,
wouldn't you like to use one of the fine needles that I got as a
present from you?"—"No, this needle will get into all the cracks
and clean my old teeth best." So now the witch poked around in
her black teeth with the poor boy!

Another time the girl had to change the youth into a bonnet,
and at once the old woman put it on and ran around with it on her
bald head for days! For this reason the young man said one day,
"Fenchelchen, this is no place for you and me—we must run away!"

Thus, here the old sorceress is making fun of the young
couple, not in words, but in deeds in the manner of the genuine
folk fairy tale, where humor does not generally consist in witty
dialogue but in amusing developments in the plot. In numerous
French variants, the two lovers deceive the old fairy, who keeps a
parrot as a lookout. Now when the handsome prince arrives and
is hiding from the witch under a lace handkerchief, the parrot
screeches, "Godmother! Godmother, the prince is under the
lace!" But Persinette is ready with an explanation, and now the
witch wants to test the parrot. "What kind of weather did we
have today?" she asks. Persinette, however, has anticipated such
a question and poured water past the parrot's window. The
parrot answers the fairy, "It rained."—"You are a liar," the fairy
says. The next day Persinette lets flour fall past the parrot's
window, and now the latter asserts that it has snowed. The third
day Persinette deceives the bird with peas. It tells the fairy it has
hailed, so that she again thinks the bird is lying, and the crafty

couple remain undisturbed for the time being. In the Italian variants, no parrots appear, but instead there is the popular motif of the talking household effects.

> In the witch's house everything could speak, even the bricks. For this reason Vermiglia asked the prince to help her make two or three bowls of macaroni, and when she had cooked it she served it spoon by spoon to all the objects. . . . Now when the old woman came home she was not able to find Vermiglia anywhere. She asked all the objects in the house, but none of them would tell, because they had been given the macaroni. But Vermiglia had forgotten a saucepan behind the door, and this saucepan tattled. It told the old woman that Vermiglia had given them all macaroni to keep them quiet but it—the saucepan—had been overlooked. The old woman became furious and threw the saucepan on the floor, shouting, "And if she had given you macaroni you would not have said anything either!" And the witch leaped out of the window in order to catch up with the fugitives.

The unpretentious folk tales are full of such sport. Let us see what finally happens in Malta as Fenchelchen, and Petersilchen, flee from pursuers. In both versions, the girl takes along with her balls of magic yarn from the magic tower, and these provide obstacles which detain the old woman. When Petersilchen throws the green one on the ground, a big garden springs up, and the gardener pretends to be deaf. The witch addresses him, saying:

> "My friend, did you not see a youth and maiden fleeing past?" —"Cabbage is very inexpensive this year!" The old woman was angered and repeated the question. "Yes, cauliflower is very reasonable, too. For half a soldo I'll give you a big head that's firm and white!"—"You fool! Were the fugitives running toward the place where the sun rises?"—"Vegetables can't grow without the sun!" Now old Aula lost her patience and ran off without further delay. And although the fugitives had a considerable head start already, she almost succeeded in overtaking the couple.

The ball of blue yarn becomes a sea which the witch swims across with great effort. The red ball turns into a fire in which the

pursuer finally perishes. As in "Hansel and Gretel," evil is over-
some in its own element: the sorceress's own magic turns against
her. Petersilchen, however, can now marry the prince; all bad
magic has an end. When we glance back over all the variants of
the Rapunzel fairy tale, we are struck not only be the good mood
in which they are told and how many flashes of wit they produce,
but also by the fact that the conclusion is always different than it
is in the version of the Grimm brothers. Only in the Grimm version do we read that the heroine, cast out into the wilderness,
gives birth to a pair of twins, and that her prince, in despair,
jumps from the window, loses his eyes, and only after many years
is healed again by Rapunzel's two tears. This could be the sentimental invention of an era that reveled in emotion. And, indeed,
it can be shown that the Grimm brothers did not draw here on
popular tales but found the entire Rapunzel tale, with all its
elaborate detail, in the work of an eighteenth-century novelist.
The Grimm brothers thought this novelist had heard the fairy
tale told by the common people and had then greatly embellished and expanded it. They believed one had only to condense
it and purify it in order to regain a good German fairy tale, the
version which now appears in their collection. In reality, the
eighteenth-century German text was only a translation of a
French fairy tale composed by a lady in waiting at the court of
Louis XIV in the year 1698 and based on a French folk fairy tale.
The concluding section has no parallel among genuine folk fairy
tales and is an invention of the lady in waiting, Mademoiselle de
la Force. The Grimm brothers accepted the conclusion with some
reluctance, still in the belief that it was a modified version of a
German folk fairy tale. In this they were mistaken. The genuine
folk fairy tales conclude with the so-called "magic escape," in
which the pursuer is three times hampered or led astray by some
magical obstacle and is finally rendered harmless. This is the
clear fairy-tale structure, with its three-beat rhythm: every stage is
clearly separated from the other, and each obstacle appears in a
different form. The genuine fairy tale appeals to the listener's
feeling for form, his ability to visualize, and his sense of rhythm.
It also has room for humor, something one cannot detect in the

Grimm version of the Rapunzel tale. The name Rapunzel, moreover, appeared in the story for the first time in the above-mentioned eighteenth-century translation. In the French fairy tale of Mademoiselle de la Force, the heroine was still called Persinette. Thus, much in the Grimm version is not genuine. And yet how captivating it is! It is compelling proof of their storytelling genius that they were able to create from their ornate model one of the most popular fairy tales in their collection. They have translated the seventeenth-century fairy tale back into the style of the folk fairy tale. And the lines they composed, "Rapunzel, Rapunzel, let thy hair down," sound so archaic and magical that they were for a long time thought to be a remnant of a very early stage and testimony to the great age of this particular tale. The Grimm version is recent, but the other variants we have seen go back to ancient folk fairy tales which have been passed down by word of mouth from century to century, whose origins are lost in the darkness of past ages, and about whose authors we know nothing.

CHAPTER 9

THE RIDDLE PRINCESS

Cunning, Jest, and Sagacity

One of the basic themes in our fairy tales is battle. The hero has to conquer a dragon or some other monster, an evil sorcerer, a witch, or a band of robbers. In a modern Greek fairy tale, it is a squat little fellow who opposes the prince.

> He was five spans tall and his teeth were two spans long; for this reason they called him "Dontá" or the toothy one. When the prince saw how small he was, he laughed and came down from his castle in order to slay him. But Dontá clicked his teeth together and brought forth ten armed men out of his mouth who looked just like him. And the battle began. The prince slew all ten, but Dontá clicked his teeth together again and forty armed men leaped from his mouth and they all did battle with the prince. That was too much for the poor prince, and Dontá slew him and took the king's daughter for himself.

The prince is brought back to life again, and in a new and different type of contest finally conquers the uncanny Dontá. He is helped in this by the cunning of the king's daughter.

In the evening when Dontá had returned from hunting and they had eaten, the princess asked him, "If you love me, tell me how wealthy you are and where you get the power to bring armed men out of your mouth." Dontá laughed and told her, "Is that any concern of yours? Very well, my strength is in this broom." The girl did not believe him, but picked up the broom, dressed it up in her finest clothes, and fondled it and kissed it like a person. Dontá laughed loudly. "You hypocrite," he said to her, "why do you dress the broom up like that? Is it a person?" And he said, "Up on those mountains there lives a wild boar, and this is where my strength comes from. When the boar gets sick, so do I, and if someone should slay it I would become incurably ill. In its stomach are three doves. If two of them should be killed I could no longer move my hands and feet, and if three were killed then I would die."

And now our prince knows how to get the better of the loathsome Dontá. The folk fairy tales take special delight in telling of the metamorphosis contest between the evil sorcerer and his pupil. In this contest, the sorcerer and his apprentice transform themselves, by turns, into various animals, and the bigger one always tries to eat up the smaller one. Finally, the youth becomes a handful of seeds, and the sorcerer, in the form of a rooster, picks up one after the other. The last little grain of seed, however, suddenly assumes the form of a hawk and finishes off the rooster.

The great role played by combats and contests in the fairy tale has led to the assumption that these stories originated in the sphere of knightly society. However, combat is a basic element of human existence in general, and its ceremonious expression in knighthood is only the especially striking stylization of a phenomenon common to all men. The fairy tale's fondness for portraying battles can be explained by its tendency to incorporate the basic themes of human existence and by its love of action. The fairy tale is an epic genre: it portrays external events. But unexpectedly the conflict enters the psychological realm. The dreadful Dontá can be conquered not by physical force, but by cunning, i.e., by psychological force. Hansel and Gretel, too, overcome the witch through cunning. Hansel holds a little bone

out through the bars of his stall instead of his finger, to show that
he is not yet fat enough to slaughter. And Gretel asks the witch to
show her how to crawl into the oven. In the French version of the
Rapunzel tale in which the witch uses a parrot as a lookout, the
girl fools both the old woman and her parrot. In these examples,
cleverness and mental dexterity are involved; in a number of
others, the so-called "riddle fairy tales," these qualities move to
the forefront. The tales concern people who propound riddles
and those who solve them. The most beloved and best known is
the figure of the riddle princess, who either asks or solves riddles.
The Persian fairy tale concerning Turandot has inspired writers
and composers. Carlo Gozzi in the eighteenth century and
Friedrich Schiller in the early nineteenth century both wrote
Turandot dramas; Giacomo Puccini wrote a Turandot opera in
the twentieth century, and in Bertolt Brecht's literary remains
there is a revision of the Schiller drama. Turnadot does not want
to marry. She confronts all her suitors with a series of riddles, and
if they are unable to solve them, they lose their heads. Finally,
Prince Kalaf comes, and he is able to answer all three questions
correctly.

> "Tell me, what is at home in every country, is every man's
> friend and cannot tolerate its equal?"—"Oh, my lady," answered
> Kalaf, "that is the sun."—"He is right," cried all the scholars, "it is
> the sun." The princess continued: "What mother sends her chil-
> dren out into the world and when they have become full-grown
> devours them?"—"The sea," answered the Prince of the Nogaits,
> "for the rivers which flow into the sea also had their origin there."

As Turandot asks the last question, she lifts the veil from her
radiantly beautiful face in order to distract the prince—but he is
victorious a third time.

> "What tree has leaves which are all white on one side and all
> black on the other?"—"The tree," said Kalaf, "is the year—which
> consists of days and nights."

So goes the Persian tale. In Schiller's drama, the questions
are somewhat different; moreover, they are declaimed in lengthy

strophes full of poetic images. In a number of respects, however, Schiller brings out very nicely the spirit of the fairy tale—for example, in the introductory note in which he speaks of the poles at the city gate, "on top of which several shorn heads with Turkish forelocks are set up symmetrically in the form of *masks*, so that they can be viewed as decoration." The unrealistic, sublimating manner of the fairy tale, which stylizes frightful things, turns them into ornamentation, and thus deprives them of their reality, is here made clearly evident. Interesting are the reflections which Schiller has one of the courtiers express:

> Another woman would have sent her suitors
> On perilous and blood-stained missions of
> Adventure, to engage in fights with giants,
> Or for three molar teeth to be extracted
> At dinner from the Shah of Babylon,
> Or to obtain for her the dancing water
> Or the singing tree, or the bird that talks—
> But nothing of the sort! What she dotes on
> Is *riddles*! Three nice questions neatly posed!
> While on them you can stay all warm and cozy
> At home without so much as ever getting
> Your shoes wet. Sword need never leave its sheath,
> But wit and cunning must be up and doing.

These lines precisely describe a process belonging to the fairy tale as such. To be sure, the fairy tale likes to portray external happenings. It does not portray feelings, moods, inner conflicts, and thought processes, but strives to translate everything into action. It doesn't tell us that the third son is compassionate and truthful, but shows him as he shares his bread with a beggar and kindly gives him the information he seeks, whereas the older brothers keep their cake for themselves and answer the question with derision and lies. The fairy tale has that "regal privilege" of which Carl Spitteler speaks, the privilege of the epic "to transform everything into action." And precisely because the fairy tale does not psychologize but portrays external happenings truly and clearly, these actions acquire a transparency and brilliance which one

seeks in vain in other types of narrative. The fairy tale depicts
external events, but these events seem to become spiritualized
and sublimated almost by themselves. The favorites of the fairy
tale are not herdsmen or blacksmiths, but kings and princesses; it
does not concern coal or grain, but gold, silver, and glass. Thus, it
is not surprising that the motif of the contest can also be sublimated in the form of a riddle contest. The fairy-tale style, which
has such a great preference for sharp lines—swords, rings, castles,
passages, little boxes, chambers, and stiff clothing—also has a special
liking for the sharp contest between two good minds. The fairy
tale has a liking for what is clearly formed and developed. In this
sense, the miracle in the fairy tale is also just an ultimate consequence of the over-all manner of presentation.

Schiller has his Turandot give a detailed explanation for her
actions:

> There still is time, Prince. Give it up! Give up
> This reckless undertaking!
> God knows those tongues are liars that accuse
> Me of hard-heartedness and cruelty.
> Hard I am not. I merely want my freedom.
> I won't be someone else's creature. I,
> An emperor's daughter, shall assert this right
> Which is innate in every human being,
> Even the lowliest, from its mother's womb.
> Across the whole of Asia I see woman
> Debased and to a slavish yoke condemned,
> And I shall take revenge for my offended sex
> Upon this haughty race of menfolk who
> Have no advantage over gentler women
> Save raw, crude strength. Upon me Nature has
> Conferred the weapon of inventive wit
> And ingenuity to guard my freedom.
> I want to have nothing to do with men.
> I hate them. I despise their haughty pride
> And superciliousness. Toward everything
> That's precious they reach out with greedy hands;
> Whatever strikes their fancy they must have.
> If Nature has endowed me with some charms

> And given me intelligence, why must
> It always be the lot of noble things
> To rouse the huntsman to the hunt, when baser things
> Hide quietly in their unworthiness?
> Must beauty be a prey that only one
> Man captures? It is free, free as the sun,
> The glorious, all-rejoicing sun in heaven,
> The fountainhead of light, all eyes' enjoyment,
> But no man's slave or private property.

Here, Schiller forsakes the fairy-tale style. Fairy-tale figures do not talk so much, and that is not a disadvantage. The true fairy-tale princess acts out of inner necessity. She need not explain her actions; she is not doing battle with the customs of Asia. With his brilliant words, Schiller destroys the delightful naturalness of the action. Here, we feel why the events and characters in the genuine folk fairy tale have such a strong, symbolic appeal. The principal actors in the fairy tale are neither individuals nor character types, but merely figures, and for just this reason can stand for a great many things. One can view them as representatives of cosmic or psychic forces just as easily as real people. Turandot's rationalistic self-appraisal in the Schiller drama, however, at once narrows the sphere of signification of this figure. It now appears almost entirely as a private individual with special problems and talents. In the fairy tale, the riddle princess remains purely a figure: she can be viewed either as a person or as a symbol for the world, which presents us with its difficult riddles and threatens to destroy us if we cannot solve them.

The content alone of Turandot's three questions suggest that things of a cosmic significance are involved. The answer to the riddle of the sphinx in the Greek Oedipus legend is *man*; but the answers to Turandot's questions are the *sun*, the *sea*, and the *year*. This transcending of the human realm is in the nature of the fairy tale. The sun, the sea, and the tree that stands for the year are large, clear symbols such as the fairy tale loves; they direct attention to the all-encompassing cosmos in which man moves. We immediately realize that this is not just a peculiarity of the Turandot tale when we look at other riddle fairy tales. The farcical fairy tale about the peasant's clever daughter is widely known and may serve as an example. In many variants, there is a quarrel between two farmers—over a field, for instance, or a cow. The judge will decide in favor of whoever gives good answers to his riddles. Now the rich, wicked farmer answers wrongly each time; but the poor, innocent farmer, prompted by his clever daughter, has the correct answers. The judge asks, "What is the fattest (*Trans. note.* German *fett* can mean either "greasy" or "fertile.") thing in the world?" The rich man answers, "bacon," but the peasant's daughter, "The earth." Again the judge asks, "What is the sweetest thing in the world?" The rich man replies, "Honey," but the clever girl, "Sleep." What is the whitest thing in the world? Not milk, as the peasant answers, but the sun. And the highest? Not the church steeple, but the stars. The rich farmer remains in the sphere of his surroundings and possessions, but the clever girl considers the world in its entirety. Here, too, the clever peasant girl is probably not interpreted exclusively as a real person. She can be viewed as a force in the spirit of the poor peasant.

Most riddle fairy tales manage to do without magic and miracles. They are therefore classified as so-called "novella fairy tales." However, they, too, are genuine fairy tales, unrealistic and stylized, but rich in images and symbols and having the tendency to encompass the world. That riddles are not extraneous elements in them is shown very nicely in a delightful fairy tale from Brittany. The beginning reads as follows:

> There once was a king of France who had a daughter who did nothing all day long but solve riddles and difficult problems of all sorts. She became so adept at this that she could find nothing at all that was difficult enough for her. Every problem she was presented with, no matter how complicated or obscure, was for her child's play.
>
> Now one day she let it be known throughout the kingdom: whoever could present her with a riddle that she could not solve in three days she would take as a husband, no matter who it was; but if she could solve the riddle, the man would forfeit his life.

And now from all over the kingdom and even from distant lands there came a great throng of suitors. All sorts of people came —princes and tailors and charcoal burners—and they all considered their riddles unsolvable. The princess stood on a balcony high above the courtyard in the royal palace. She was dressed in a red robe, had a golden crown on her head and wore a diamond star on her forehead. In her hand she carried a white staff, and she gazed down with a look as arrogant and cruel as that of a tyrant. All around the courtyard on the walls and on poles were the bodies and skeletons of her victims. The princess usually gave her answers at once from up on the balcony and immediately the poor suitor was seized and mercilessly hanged by four fierce-looking servants.

Now in Brittany there lives a young nobleman by the name of Fanch de Kerbrinic. He is not exactly the cleverest person in the world, but he wants nevertheless to go and propose a riddle for the princess. One day he meets a shrewd fellow, a soldier who goes by the name of Petit-Jean. He confides in him and tells him his plan, and Petit-Jean asks just what sort of riddle he has prepared. The nobleman has, as a precaution, thought up two of them and now tries them out by reciting them to the soldier.

> Guess, what do I throw over the house
> While the end remains in my hand.

"A ball of yarn," Petit-Jean answered, laughing. "That is much too easy; a five-year-old child could guess that. Now the other riddle!"

> I throw one over the house,
> I go to see and there find three.

"An egg! When it breaks one finds the white, the yolk and the shell—those are the three. No, that's not any good; it won't do if you wish to match wits with the princess. But take me with you, follow my advice exactly and I guarantee you will succeed."

The nobleman's mother wants to keep her son at home, and when her pleas are to no avail, gives him and his companion two glasses of a strong poison before they leave. But Petit-Jean senses danger and outwits the noblewoman by pouring the potion in their horses' ears. Toward evening, the horses suddenly fall down dead. Four magpies—in other variants, they are ravens—fall upon them, and the poisoned horseflesh kills them as well. Now Petit-Jean takes the dead magpies along and, in the next village, has them baked into eight little cakes. Later, our two friends come upon sixteen robbers in a dreaded forest. The robbers invite them to dinner, and our friends show their thanks by offering them their eight magpie cakes. The robbers eat them, turn around, and fall down dead. And now Petit-Jean knows what to ask the princess.

When they were still around twelve miles from Paris, Petit-Jean said to his friend, "Now we shall soon be in Paris; we must think about our undertaking. Have you thought up a riddle yet which you can ask the princess and that won't be just child's play for her?"—"I only know what I have already told you," answered Monsieur de Kerbrinic. "Then I will tell you one; pay close attention and try to remember. You must tell the princess, 'When we left home we were four. Of the four, two died. From the two, four died. From the four, we made eight. From the eight, sixteen died, and now four of us again come to you.' Do you understand?"—"No, upon my soul, I don't understand a word. Please explain to me what all that might mean."—"Nothing is simpler. When we departed from your castle we were four in number—you, I and our two horses."—"Correct."—"Of the four, two died—our two horses who died from the poison we poured in their ears when we left." —"I see."—"From the two, four died—the four magpies that we found dead the next morning by the horses."—"Quite so."— "From the four we made eight—the eight cakes that we poisoned with the four magpies."—"Aha!"—"From the eight, sixteen died —the sixteen robbers who were poisoned by the cakes and died." —"That is true."—"And now four of us again come to you— we bought two horses with the money we took from the robbers, and now the two of them plus the two of us make four again, just as we were when we left your castle. Isn't that clear?"—"Clear as day! And yet the princess will never guess!"—"Now repeat the riddle for me, for you must learn it so you can tell it to the princess."—"Yes, I will repeat it for you. Nothing is simpler: when we left home, we were four. Of the four, two died. From the two, three died—"—"No, no, that's not right. Listen again, and then repeat it right after me." Petit-Jean recited the riddle again very quickly. Kerbrinic tried to repeat it after him, but again got all mixed up. The rest of the journey he practiced and practiced and after they arrived in Paris he needed two more days until he could tell it and explain it properly. On the third day Petit-Jean said to him, "Very well, now go to the palace, ask them to take you before the princess, and give her the riddle. But take care that you don't make any mistakes."—"Never fear: I can recite it and explain it now as well as you can."

This Breton tale shows the characteristic style of French fairy tales, which often have something ironic about them. They are not as ingenuous as German fairy tales and not as earthy as the Russian; playful elegance and at the same time a certain realism enter in. The scene for our fairy tale is not some unspecified locale; it begins at a precisely designated Breton estate and gravitates toward the focal point of everything French—Paris. And the servant is more clever than his master; this comes close to being a humorous sort of social criticism. One hardly thinks of anything like this in the tale of the clever peasant girl who outwits not only the king and the wealthy peasant, but her own poor father as well. One thing, however, the Breton tale has in common with the countless variants known all over the world: the riddle is derived from the fairy-tale plot. Just as in other fairy tales, the hero sets forth full of confidence to perform some task, although he has no idea how he will do it, here Petit-Jean has confidence that his journey will bring the right thing to mind. In other fairy tales, a little man or a talking animal presents the hero with the crucial advice or the magic object which helps him; here, the action itself performs the same service for the clever soldier. The Grimm brothers believed that fairy tales are not consciously created but in a certain sense create themselves. The fact that in our tale and in its numerous variants the riddle shapes itself is a striking confirmation of their views. The nobleman's consciously contrived riddles are worthless, but the riddle which is created by itself is victorious: naturally, the princess cannot solve it. The fairy tale, with its love of action, derives the riddle as well from the plot—an unexpected but logical consequence of its style.

Thus, the riddle is not a foreign substance in the fairy tale. It is firmly embedded in the totality and conforms to the style of the tale. The fairy tale and the riddle are essentially related. There are dialects which use the same word for both—those of Lorraine and the region around Eger in northwest Bohemia, for example. In both fairy tale and riddle, one senses something hidden and mysterious, and yet both are at the same time gay and playful in nature. The origins of the riddle are, like those of the fairy tale, a matter of controversy. Are the roots to be found ultimately in secret religious cults which posed for their neophytes difficult riddles concerning the mysteries of the world? Is the existence of riddles as a genre an indication that man views his life and the world as a riddle? Or are riddles just the playful expression of an agile mind delighting in its own resourcefulness? The impartial observer certainly will detect some of each in both the riddle and the fairy tale. And both the endeavors to probe the mysteries of existence and the joy in artistic creation no doubt played a role in the origin of both riddle and fairy tale. Riddles and fairy tales —or stories similar to fairy tales—are at home among all peoples of the world. There are peoples with a special talent for inventing fairy tales; likewise, there are peoples with a talent for riddles. One finds a delight in telling and solving difficult riddles and the like especially among the people of India. In their tales subtle questions are often posed. For example, if a woman's husband and her lover are both beheaded, whose wife is she when both are brought back to life, if the heads are interchanged? The correct answer is not the one with her husband's head, but the one with the head of her lover. Why? "In the marriage ceremony the man offers the bride his right hand, and this is part of the torso." It is quite possible that such riddle tales have traveled from India to Persia, North Africa, and Europe, but not every riddle fairy tale can be traced back to India: the delight in inventing and solving riddles is found among all peoples. The principals are not always princesses or peasant girls. Clever lads and simple men often appear. One need only think of the well-known humorous tale of the emperor and the abbot in which the abbot's shepherd dons his master's cowl, appears before the emperor, and gives brilliant answers to his captious questions ("How high is the sky? How deep is the sea? How much am I worth?"—or the like). Here, too, the servant is more clever than his master, the shepherd cleverer than the abbot, and the potter more so than the vizier; but this does not have the effect of social criticism, primarily, but has a wider, symbolic significance. Just as in the case of Cinderella, the Simpleton or the Mangy Little Horse, that which is insignificant and despised unexpectedly proves itself to be the really valuable person or thing. In this sense, many fairy-tale figures are really riddle figures: they are not what they appear to be. Cinderella is, in her own way, the embodied riddle princess: she presents the prince with a riddle, not in words but in her appearance. This riddle he is finally able to solve, again not by words, but through his actions.

Fairy tales have always had a special attraction for writers and poets, and riddle fairy tales seem to have had an exceptionally strong appeal. Gozzi, Schiller, and Brecht wrote Turandot dramas. In our times, Carl Orff has dramatized and set to music the Grimm brothers' version of "The Clever Peasant Girl," and the heroine of our humorous fairy tale now appears on the opera stage with the name *"Die Kluge"* (the clever one). Shakespeare, in the *Merchant of Venice,* has the suitors of the beautiful Portia confronted with a riddle, as is the title hero of *Pericles* often attributed to Shakespeare. In general, the tendency is to view the fairy tale as a higher form of literature that has come down to the common folk, just as one can recognize country costumes as city fashions which were taken over by the peasants. It may be that the origins of the fairy tale can be explained in such a way. One thing, however, is certain: these fairy tales circulating among the common folk have, in turn, been able to influence great literature time and again, to stimulate and renew it. For the Romantic poet Novalis, the fairy tale was nothing less than "the canon of poetry." "Everything poetic," he declared, "must be like a fairy tale." Today we would not endorse this view without reservation. But this much is evident: that the fairy tale which transforms the world, like all true poetry, is an elemental form of literature from which great writers have repeatedly drawn strength and inspiration.

CHAPTER 10

THE FAIRY-TALE HERO

The Image of Man in the Fairy Tale

Is it mere chance that the principal characters we have encountered in our studies are more often female than male: Sleeping Beauty; the Greek princess who kneaded a husband for herself out of groats, sugar, and almonds; good little Anny in the story of the little earth-cow; Rapunzel; the riddle princesses; and the clever peasant girls? The only corresponding male figures we have seen in the European fairy tales are the dragon slayer and that clever poser of riddles, Petit-Jean. Is this preponderance of women typical? Does our sampling reflect the true situation? If we are asked just which fairy-tale figures are generally best known, we immediately think of Sleeping Beauty, Cinderella, Snow White, Little Red Riding Hood, Rapunzel, The Princess in Disguise, and Goldmarie in "Mother Hulda"—all female figures. In "Hansel and Gretel" and in "Brother and Sister," the girl also plays the leading role. We find ourselves nearly at a loss when called upon for the names of male protagonists: Iron Hans and Tom Thumb, perhaps; the Brave Little Tailor, Strong Hans, and Lucky Hans—but here we are already in the realm of the folktale jest. How can one explain this peculiar predominance of women and girls? All the names mentioned are taken from the Grimm brothers' collection. Despite the existence of innumerable other collections, this one today is, in German-speaking countries, almost the sole surviving source for the public at large of real contact with the fairy tale. Now the Grimm brothers' informants were predominantly women. And today children learn fairy tales mainly from their mothers, grandmothers, aunts, and female kindergarten and school teachers. Thus, it is natural that the principal figures are mostly women. Moreover, the child—whether boy or girl—is basically closer to the feminine than the masculine, living in the domain of the mother and female teachers and not yet that of the father and male teachers. The fairy tales which grownups remember are those of their childhood. Furthermore, our era, whose character, despite everything, is still determined by men, feels the strong and clear need for a complementary antipole. The woman is assigned a privileged position, not only by social custom; in art and literature, as well, she has occupied a central position since the time of the troubadours and the Mariology of the late Middle Ages. In painting and in the novel, she has been the subject of persistent interest and loving concern. Thus, it comes as no surprise that she also plays a significant role in the fairy tale—which for centuries was one of the most vital and indirectly influential art forms in Europe—the feminine component, that part of man closer to nature, had to come to the forefront to compensate for the technological and economic system created by the masculine spirit, which dominated the external world of reality.

However, that was a peculiarity of the era. Tellers of fairy tales were not always predominantly women, and not always was existence influenced so strongly by the masculine spirit that the antipole asserted itself with such conspicuous force in art. If we go beyond *Grimm's Fairy Tales* and leaf through the many volumes of the *Märchen der Weltliteratur* (Fairy Tales of World Literature), *Das Gesicht der Völker* (The Face of the Peoples), or Richard M. Dorson's *Folktales of the World,* we see that there are at least as many masculine as feminine protagonists, and that, in general, the masculine figures may even predominate, as they do in the myths. But one thing is quite clear: at the focal point in the fairy tale stands *man*. One cannot say this of the local legend and saint's legend: they portray the intrusion of another world upon our own existence; myths tell of gods; and among primitive peoples, animal stories predominate. The hero of the European fairy tale, however, is *man*. In the minds of the ancient Greeks, the earlier animal gods assumed human form. The humanism of the Greek classical period became a basic element of European culture. Thus, a connection no doubt exists between this European or Indo-European attribute and our fairy tales, which, in the main, concern not animals, as in the stories of primitive peoples, but men.

The European fairy tale draws a picture of man and shows him in his confrontation with the world. Since our children are interested in fairy tales in their most receptive years, and since even today almost all children have a considerable number of fairy tales which are told or read to them or which they read themselves, it is worthwhile to ask what sort of picture of man they find there. Can one say that the large number of fairy tales present a coherent picture? In a certain sense, yes. The fairy-tale hero, or heroine, to be sure, is sometimes a rollicking daredevil and sometimes a silent sufferer; at times a lazybones and at times a diligent helper; often sly and wily but just as often open and honest. At times he is a shrewd fellow, an undaunted solver of riddles, a brave fighter; at others, he is a stupid person or one who sits down and begins to cry every time he encounters difficulty. There are friendly and compassionate fairy-tale heroes, but others that are merciless and perfidious. To say nothing of the differences in social class: princess and Cinderella, prince and swineherd. Or must we perhaps say something about them? Are we not perplexed by something we see at just this point? Surprisingly, the difference in social class is often only apparent. The goose-girl, in reality, is not at all one of the common folk but a princess forced into her lowly role by her servant girl. And the gardener boy with the mangy hair, whom the beautiful princess observes every morning, is, in reality, a prince who has tied an animal hide over his golden hair.

Thus, in the fairy tale, one and the same person can abruptly change from a mangy-headed youth into one with golden hair, and the despised Cinderella can suddenly turn into a dancer in a radiant gown at whom all gaze in wonder. The one considered to be stupid or loutish often turns out to be the wisest and cleverest of all. In addition, the real swineherd can unexpectedly become the princess's husband, and the poor girl can marry the prince or the king and thus be raised to royal status.

In the fairy tale, all things are possible, not just in the sense that all sorts of miracles occur, but in the sense just mentioned: the lowest can rise to the highest position, and those in the highest position—evil queens, princes, princesses, government ministers—can fall and be destroyed. It has therefore been said that fairy tales derive from the wishful thinking of poor people or those who have been unsuccessful or slighted. But such psychological and sociological interpretations are too limited. Wish dreams and wishful thinking play a part in fairy tales, just as they do in all human matters, and social tensions and yearnings also are reflected in them.

Yet these are only superficial aspects. Fairy-tale figures have an immediate appeal. The king, the princess, a dragon, a witch, gold, crystal, pitch, and ashes—these things are, for the human imagination, age-old symbols for what is high, noble, and pure or dangerous, bestial, and unfathomable; what is genuine and true, or what is sordid and false. The fairy tale often depicts how a penniless wretch becomes wealthy, a maid becomes queen, a disheveled man is changed into a youth with golden hair, or a toad, bear, ape, or dog is transformed into a beautiful maiden or handsome youth. Here, we feel at once the capacity for change of man in general. The focal point is not the rise of the servant to his position of master, not the esteem and recognition accorded the former outcast child; these are images for something more fundamental: man's deliverance from an unauthentic existence and his commencement of a true one. When the real princess lets herself be forced into the role of a goose girl while the lowly maid arrogates to herself the dominant position, this means that a false, ignoble side of the total personality gains control and suppresses that which is truly regal. When the prince marries the witch's ugly daughter instead of his bride-to-be, he has lost the way to his own soul and given himself up to a strange demon. The psychologist views things in this way, assuming that the fairy tale depicts processes within the mind. Although such specialized interpretations are often risky, it is evident that more is involved for both the author and his hearers than mere external action when the fairy tale tells how the hero conquers the dragon, marries the princess, and becomes king.

In general, one can say that the fairy tale depicts processes of development and maturation. Every man has within him an ideal image, and to be king, to wear a crown, is an image for the ascent into the highest attainable realms. And every man has within him his own secret kingdom. The visible kingdom, the figure of the princess and her bridegroom, are fascinating, influential, and oft-cited even in democratic societies because they have a symbolic force. To be king does not mean just to have power; in the modern world, kings and queens have been relieved of almost all their material power. One might say they have been freed of it and by this have acquired even greater symbolic appeal. To be a king is an image for complete self-realization; the crown and royal robe which play such a great role in the fairy tale make visible the splendor and brilliance of the great perfection achieved inwardly. They call to mind an analogous phenomenon in the saint's legend, the halo, which likewise renders visible the inward brilliance. When Gold-marie, after proving herself in the realm of Mother Hulda, is showered with gold, no one doubts that this is an image—one which reveals the girl's good soul. And when other fairy-tale heroines comb golden flowers out of their hair, or when a flower shoots out of the ground at their every step, we likewise immediately take it to be symbolic. Not only alchemists, but people generally feel gold to be a representative for a higher human and cosmic perfection. Kingship, like gold and the royal robe, has symbolic significance and power in the fairy tale. It may well be—as psychologists of the Jungian school assert—that the marriage with the animal bride or animal prince, the union of the

king with the armless mute lost in the forest, and the wedding of
the princess and the goatherd are images for the union of dispar-
ities in the human soul, for the awareness of a hitherto unrecog-
nized spiritual strength, and for the maturation into a complete
human personality. In any event, the fairy tale depicts over and
over an upward development, the overcoming of mortal dangers
and seemingly insoluble problems, the path toward marriage
with the prince or princess, toward kingship or gold and jewels.
The image of man portrayed in the fairy tale—or, rather, one
aspect of this image—is that of one who has the capability to rise
above himself, has within him the yearning for the highest things,
and is also able to attain them. We can be sure that children,
engrossed in the story as it is told to them, do not understand this
in all its implications; but, what is more important, they can
sense it. The child, at the fairy-tale age, is fascinated not by the
upward social movement but by the overcoming of dangers and
entry into the realm of glory, whether this is depicted as the
realm of the sun and stars or as an earthly kingdom of unearthly
splendor.

But the image of man as it appears in the fairy tale can be
defined from yet another aspect upon closer examination. The
fairy-tale hero is essentially a wanderer. Whereas the events in the
local legend usually take place in the hometown or its vicinity,
the fairy tale time and again sends its heroes out into the world.
Sometimes the parents are too poor to be able to keep their children, at times the hero is forced away by a command or enticed
away by a contest, or it may be merely that the hero decides to go
out in search of adventure. In a Low German fairy tale, the
father sends his two eldest sons out into the world as punishment,
but does the same thing to his youngest son as a reward. Nothing
shows more clearly that the fairy tale will use any excuse to make
its hero a wanderer and lead him far away, often to the stars, to
the bottom of the sea, to a region below the earth, or to a kingdom at the end of the world. The female protagonist is also frequently removed to a distant castle or abducted to that place by
an animal-husband. This wandering, or soaring, over great dis-
tances conveys an impression of freedom and ease that is further

strengthened by other characteristics in the fairy tale which also convey a feeling of freedom. Whereas in the local legends man is endowed from the very beginning with something stifling and unfree by stagnation in the ancestral village and dumbfounded gazing at the frightful phenomenon, the fairy-tale hero appears as a free-moving wanderer. In the local legend, man is an impassioned dreamer, a visionary; the fairy-tale hero, however, strides from place to place without much concern or astonishment. The other worldly beings which he encounters interest him only as helpers or opponents and do not inspire him with either curiosity, a thirst for knowledge, or a vague fear of the supernatural. The fairy tale depicts its heroes not as observing and fearful but as moving and active. In the local legend, man is embedded in the society of his village, not only that of the living, but also that of the dead. He is also rooted in the countryside or town in which he lives. The wild people in the forest and the mountains and the water sprites and poltergeists inhabit the general surroundings. The fairy-tale hero, however, breaks away from his home and goes out into the world. He is almost always alone; if there are two brothers, they separate at a certain crossroads and each experiences the decisive adventure alone. Frequently the fairy-tale hero does not return to his home town. When he sets forth to save a king's daughter or accomplish a difficult task, he usually does not know how he will accomplish his purpose. But along the way he meets a little old man, shares his bread with him, and gets from him the advice that will lead him to his goal. Or he meets a wild animal, pulls out a thorn that was hurting it, and thus gains the help of the thankful beast, whose abilities just suffice to solve his problem. In the local legend, people summon the priest or Capuchin to help in conjuring spirits, but the fairy-tale hero enters strange lands all alone and there has the decisive confrontation. The priest or Capuchin is not only a member of the village community, everyone knows the source of his helping powers: the salvation of the Christian church, the grace of God. The helping animals and other supernatural beings in the fairy tale are, however, usually just as isolated as the fairy-tale hero himself. The latter takes their advice and magic gifts noncha-

lantly, uses them at the decisive moment, and then no longer
thinks about them. He doesn't ponder over the mysterious forces
or where his helpers have come from; everything he experiences
seems natural to him and he is carried along by this help, which
he has earned often without his knowledge. The fairy-tale hero
quite frequently is the youngest son, an orphan, a despised
Cinderella or poor goatherd, and this all contributes to making
the hero appear isolated; the prince, princess, and king, as well,
at the very pinnacle of society, are in their own way detached,
absolute, and isolated.   *look at yearsly p. 212*

Local legends and fairy tales, which have existed for centuries side by side among the common folk, complement one
another. Local legends originate among the common people half
spontaneously and half under the influence of simple traditions
and ask, we might say, the anxious question, "What is man, what
is the world?" Fairy tales certainly do not originate among simple
folk but with great poets, perhaps the so-called "initiated," or
religious, poets; and, in a sense, they provide an answer. In the
local legend, one senses the anxiety of man, who, though apparently a part of the community of his fellow men, finds himself
ultimately confronted with an uncanny world which he finds
hard to comprehend and which threatens him with death. The
fairy tale, however, presents its hero as one who, though not com-
prehending ultimate relationships, is led safely through the dangerous, unfamiliar world. The fairy-tale hero is gifted, in the
literal sense of the word. Supernatural beings lavish their gifts on
him and help him through battles and perils. In the fairy tale,
too, the ungifted, the unblessed, appear. Usually, they are the
older brothers or sisters of the hero or heroine. They are often
deceitful, wicked, envious, cold-hearted, or dissolute—though this
is by no means always the case. It may be that they just don't
come across any helping animal or little man; they are the unblessed. The hearer does not, however, identify with them, but
with the hero, who makes his way through the world alone—and
for just this reason is free and able to establish contact with essential things. Usually, it is his unconsciously correct behavior that
gains him the help of the animal with the magic powers or some

other supernatural creature. This behavior, however, need not be moral in the strict sense. The idler is also a favorite of the fairy tale; it may be that he is given the very thing he wants and needs most: that his every wish is fulfilled without his having to move a finger. In the fairy tale about the frog-king, the heroine who repeatedly tries to avoid keeping her promise and finally flings the irksome frog against the wall in order to kill it is neither kind, compassionate, nor even dutiful. But by flinging the frog against the wall, she has, without knowing it, fulfilled the secret conditions for the release of the enchanted prince who had been transformed into a frog. The hero and heroine in the fairy tale do the right thing, they hit the right key; they are heaven's favorites. The local legend, provided it is not jesting in tone, usually portrays man as unblessed, unsuccessful, and as one who, despite his deep involvement in the community, must face life's ultimate questions alone and uncertain. The fairy tale sees man as one who is essentially isolated but who, for just this reason—because he is not rigidly committed, not tied down—can establish relationships with anything in the world. And the world of the fairy tale includes not just the earth, but the entire cosmos. In the local legend, man is seemingly integrated in the community, but inwardly, essentially, he is alone. The fairy-tale hero is seemingly isolated, but has the capacity for universal relationships. Certainly, we can say that both are true portrayals of man. The local legend expresses a basic human condition: although deeply entrenched in human institutions, man feels abandoned, cast into a threatening world which he can neither understand nor view as a whole. The fairy tale, however, which also knows of failure and depicts it in its secondary characters, shows in its heroes that, despite our ignorance of ultimate things, it is possible to find a secure place in the world. The fairy-tale hero also does not perceive the world as a whole, but he puts his trust in and is accepted by it. As if led by an invisible force and with the confidence of a sleepwalker, he follows the right course. He is isolated and at the same time in touch with all things. The fairy tale is a poetic vision of man and his relationship to the world, a vision that for centuries inspired the fairy tale's hearers with strength and confidence because they sensed the fundamental truth of this vision. Even though man may feel outcast and abandoned in the world, like one groping in the dark, is he not in the course of his life led from step to step and guided safely by a thousand aids? The fairy tale, however, not only inspires trust and confidence; it also provides a sharply defined image of man: isolated, yet capable of universal relationships. It is salutary that in our era, which has experienced the loss of individuality, nationalism, and impending nihilism, our children are presented with just such an image of man in the fairy tales they hear and absorb. This image is all the more effective for having proceeded naturally from the over-all style of the fairy tale. The fairy-tale technique—the sharp lines, the two-dimensional, sublimating portrayal we have so often observed as well as he capsuling of the individual episodes and motifs—this entire technique is isolating, and only for this reason can it interconnect all things so effortlessly. The image of man in the fairy tale, the figure of the hero, grows out of its over-all style; this gives it a persuasive power which cannot fail to impress even the realistically minded listener.

Every type of fairy tale portrays events which can safely be interpreted as images for psychological or cosmic processes. Every single fairy tale has a particular message. A beautiful girl's eyes are cruelly torn out and then, one year and a day later, are replaced and can see seven times as clearly as before. Another fairy-tale heroine is locked up in a box by her wicked mother-in-law and hung in the chimney, where she remains without nourishment until her husband returns from the war; yet the smoked woman does not die of hunger—indeed, she emerges from her box younger and more beautiful. Such stories make the listener feel how suffering can purify and strengthen. In speaking of the wisdom in fairy tales, one is usually thinking of similar passages in particular fairy tales. Much more powerful, however, is the over-all image of man and the world as portrayed in folk fairy tales generally. This image recurs in a large number of tales and makes a profound impression on the listener—formerly, illiterate grownups; today, children. Is this image in accord with our present-day view of life and the world?

Modern literature, narrative as well as dramatic, is characterized by a strange turning away from the heroic figure. This begins as far back as Naturalism, where the coachman or the cleaning woman takes the place of the tragic hero, the kings and noble ladies, and where the masses—the weavers, for example—can take the place of the individual. In the modern novel, interest centers on impersonal forces, subconscious powers, and processes transcending the individual. If an individual does become the center of attention, he is often an anti-hero, or, as he is sometimes called, the passive or negative hero. The stories of Franz Kafka, which influence so much of present-day literature, have been characterized as out-and-out anti-fairy tales. And yet they have much in common with fairy tales. Their figures, like those of the fairy tale, are not primarily individuals, personalities, characters, but simply figures: doers and receivers of the action. They are no more masters of their destiny than are the figures in the fairy tale. They move through a world which they do not understand but in which they are nevertheless involved. This they have in common with the figures of the fairy tale: they do not perceive their relationship to the world about them. Whereas Kafka's figures stand helpless and despairing amidst the confusion of relationships they do not understand, the fairy-tale hero is happy in his contacts. The fairy tale is the poetic expression of the confidence that we are secure in a world not destitute of sense, that we can adapt ourselves to it and act and live even if we cannot view or comprehend the world as a whole. The preference of modern literature for the passive hero, the negative hero, is not without parallel in the fairy tale. The simpleton or dejected person who sits down on a stone and cries is not able to help himself, but help comes to him. The fairy tale, too, has a partiality for the negative hero: the insignificant, the neglected, the helpless. But he unexpectedly proves to be strong, noble, and blessed. The spirit of the folk fairy tale parallels that in modern literature to a degree, but then the listener is relieved of his feeling of emptiness and filled with confidence. The grownup, still under the influence of the Enlightenment and realism, quickly turns away from the fairy tale with a feeling of contempt. But in modern art, fascination with the fairy tale is everywhere evident. The turning away from descriptive realism, from the mere description of external reality in itself, implies an approach to the fairy tale. The same can be said of the fantastic mixtures of human, animal, vegetable, and mineral, which, like the fairy tale, bring all things into relationship with one another. Modern architecture has a great preference for what is light, bright, and transparent; one often refers to the dematerialization in architecture, the sublimation of matter. The sublimation of all material things, however, is one of the basic characteristics of fairy-tale style. We find crystal-clear description combined with elusive, mysterious meaning in fairy tales, in modern lyric poetry, and in Ernst Jünger and Franz Kafka, who has said that true reality is always unrealistic. The modern American writer W. H. Auden has said, "The sort of pleasure we get from folk fairy tales seems to me similar to that which we derive from Mallarmé's poems or from abstract painting." We are not surprised at such a statement. The fairy tale is a basic form of literature, and of art in general. The ease and calm assurance with which it stylizes, sublimates, and abstracts makes it the quintessence of the poetic process, and art in the twentieth century has again been receptive to it. We no longer view it as mere entertainment for children and those of childlike disposition. The psychologist, the pedagogue, knows that the fairy tale is a fundamental building block and an outstanding aid in development for the child; the art theorist perceives in the fairy tale—in which reality and unreality, freedom and necessity, unite—an archetypal form of literature which helps lay the groundwork for all literature, for all art. We have attempted to show, in addition, that the fairy tale presents an image of man which follows almost automatically from its over-all style. The fairy-tale style isolates and unites: its hero is thus isolated and, for this very reason, capable of entering into universal relationships. The style of the fairy tale and its image of man are of timeless validity and, at the same time, of special significance in our age. Thus, we must hope that despite the one-sided rationalistic outlook of many grownups, it will not be neglected and forgotten by our children and by the arts.

CHAPTER 11

THE MIRACLE
IN LITERATURE

If we take the word "miracle" in the broad sense of an intrusion of something supernatural into ordinary reality, we can say that, from the very start, the miracle played an important role in literature. Ancient myths concerned themselves with the wondrous deeds of gods and deified men, and these myths live on in the great epics of civilized peoples. The situation is similar in the drama, which in both classical times and in the Middle Ages developed from liturgy. In medieval European drama, the Easter play celebrated the miracle of Christ's resurrection, the Christmas pageant commemorated the miracle of His birth, and the miracle play glorified the lives of the saints. Lyric poetry, too, in its very origins was concerned with the miracle. Magic formulas which tried to bring about a miracle, usually a cure, are among the earliest literary documents in the German language. Fairy tales, saints' legends, and local legends tell of confrontations between man and supernatural beings of supernatural worlds. But not only popular literature tells of this journey to another world. The representative works of great literature in Western thought also lead their heroes into the realm of the miracle and have them enter the underworld: Homer's *Odyssey*, Vergil's *Aeneid*, Dante's *Divine Comedy*, and Goethe's *Faust*. In Goethe's time, however, the struggle set in against the dominance of the miraculous in literature. The Enlightenment led the way, and in its wake a realistic literature developed in the eighteenth and nineteenth century, which took pride in its ability to fascinate the reader without the aid of external miracles. As late as 1740 the two Swiss literary critics, Bodmer and Breitinger, characterized the miraculous as the essence of the poetic, and praised Milton's epics with their supernatural worlds. In 1779, however, Lessing's *Nathan the Wise* appeared, a dramatic poem that not only managed to do without heaven and hell, angels and devils, itself, but took an explicit stand against the traditional belief in miracles. Lessing's *Nathan* dethroned the miracle in literature and in reality, not in a frivolous way, but with reverence for God's creation. A few passages from Nathan's conversation with his daughter, Rachel, and her servant-girl, Daya, will introduce our discussion.

During the absence of her father, the rich merchant Nathan, Rachel was saved from their burning house by a young Knight Templar. Afterwards, the rescuer was nowhere to be found. For this reason, and because in her mind's eye the Knight Templar's white cape seemed like the wings of an angel, Rachel believed a miracle had occurred and tried to convince her father that she had been saved by an angel.

RACHEL.   —Have you
    Yourself not taught me that it's possible
    That there are angels, and that God can do
    Such miracles for those who love Him well?
    I love Him.
NATHAN.   And He loves you too; and does
    For you and others miracles every hour;
    Indeed, has done them from eternity
    For all of you.
RACHEL.   I like to hear that.
NATHAN.   What?

> Since it would sound quite natural, unexciting,
> If just a real and living Templar knight
> Had saved your life; would that be any less
> A miracle?—The greatest wonder is
> That to us all the true and genuine wonders
> Can come to be so commonplace, and should.
> Without this universal miracle,
> A thinking man might not have used the word
> For that which only children should so call,
> Who, gaping, only see the most uncommon,
> The latest happening.
> DAYA.   Come, Nathan, would you
> By suchlike subtleties completely shatter
> Her brain, already sadly overwrought?
> NATHAN. Leave me in peace!—Were it for Rachel then
> Not miracle enough, that by a *man*
> Her life was saved, who first by no small wonder
> Must be preserved himself? Yes, no small wonder!
> For who has ever heard that Saladin
> Had spared a Templar's life?*

"The greatest wonder is that to us all the true and genuine wonders can come to be so commonplace, and should." This is not only the essence of what Nathan has to say, it is the statement of the modern creed in general, which sees the universe as a manifestation of divine order: only childlike or obtuse minds have need of extraordinary things, miracles and signs, to be able to worship God; the mature man perceives the miraculous in everyday, ordinary, natural things. Nathan would like to bring up his daughter to be a mature person; yet he knows he cannot do this with an abstract principle. Thus, he seizes upon an objection of the servant girl, Daya:

> DAYA. What harm is there—if I may speak a word—
> In spite of all, if one should still prefer
> An angel to a man as rescuer?

* All quotations from *Nathan the Wise* are taken from the paperback edition published by Frederick Ungar.

Does one not feel thereby so much the nearer
To that mysterious First Cause of his rescue?
NATHAN. Nothing but pride! mere pride! The iron pot
Wants to be drawn with silver tongs from out
The fire, to think itself a pot of silver.—Bah!—
And what's the harm, you ask me, what's the harm?
No, what's the good, I'll ask you in return—
For your "To feel oneself the nearer God"
Is either nonsense or its's blasphemy.—
But there is harm; yes, truly, harm indeed.—
Come, hark to me!—I'm sure, to him who saved
Your life—and be it angel or a man—
You both would give, and you, my Rachel, most,
An ample service in return?—Not so?—
Well, to an angel, what's the chance that you
Can do him service, ample service, too?
Thank him you can; can sigh and pray; can melt
In ecstasy; and on his festal day
Can fast, give alms.—All futile.—For I think
In such a case you and your neighbor man
Will always gain far more than he. He grows
Not fat from all your fasting; grows not rich
With your almsgiving; gets no greater glory
From all your rapture, nor a greater power
From all your trust. Not so? But if a man!

And now, after Nathan has sharply castigated the fantasy of
his beloved daughter, branding it as pride and a sentimental
savoring of her own feelings, he does not give her time to defy
him. Still making use of his hearers' objections, he strikes the decisive blow:

NATHAN. You cruel dreamers!—Now what if this angel—
Has fallen sick? . . .
RACHEL.   Sick!
DAYA.   Sick! He won't do that!
RACHEL. What awesome chill assails me! Daya, feel!
My forehead, always warm, is turned to ice.
NATHAN. He is a Frank, not used to such a climate;

more into the background in narrative literature. The visible miracle of the verse is replaced by the less noticeable but also more differentiated beauty of the prose sentence. Nevertheless, the magic of the actual miracle is not lost to literature. Unexpectedly, such an extreme naturalist as Gerhart Hauptmann again wrote dramas in the styles of saints' legends and fairy tales: *Hanneles Himmelfahrt* (The Assumption of Hannele) and *Die versunkene Glocke* (The Sunken Bell). What was once believed can become symbolic in literature, precisely because it is no longer regarded as reality.

Thus, a work of literature, written in a time which still believed in miracles, should be meaningful to us. The audience then considered the reported events to be real and true, but at the same time no doubt sensed the symbolism.

In Shakespeare's *Macbeth,* a drama portraying a destructive tyrant on the royal throne, mention is made at one point of another ruler. Two Scotsmen who have fled the fury of the Scotch king, Macbeth, are talking with a doctor about the miracles performed by the kindly English king (act IV, scene 3):

                   —Comes the king forth, I

MALCOLM.
  pray you?
DOCTOR. Ay, sir; there are a crew of wretched souls
  That stay his cure: their malady convinces
  The great assay of art; but at his touch—
  Such sanctity hath heaven given his hand—
  They presently amend.
MALCOLM. I thank you, doctor. (Exit Doctor)
MACDUFF. What's the disease he means?
                       'Tis call'd the evil:
MALCOLM.
  A most miraculous work in this good king;
  Which often, since my here-remain in England,
  I have seen him do. How he solicits heaven,
  Himself best knows: but strangely-visited people,
  All swoln and ulcerous, pitiful to the eye,
  The mere despair of surgery, he cures,
  Hanging a golden stamp about their necks,
  Put on with holy prayers: and 'tis spoken,

  Is young; to tasks demanded by his order,
  To hunger, waking, little used.
RACHEL.   Sick, sick!
DAYA. It's possible, that's all that Nathan means.
NATHAN. Now there he lies, has neither friend nor coin
  To pay for friendliness.
RACHEL.   O dear, my father!
NATHAN. Lies without tending, comfort, or advice,
  A prey to pain and death!
RACHEL.   Where, where?
NATHAN.   And he,
  Who for a girl he'd never known nor seen—
  Enough that she was human—plunged in fire. . . .
DAYA.   O spare her, Nathan!
NATHAN.   Who the girl he'd saved
  Would not approach or see again, to save
  Her thanking him. . . .
DAYA.   O spare her, Nathan!
NATHAN.   Nor
  Desired to see her more—unless it were
  That he a second time should save her life,—
  Being a human soul. . . .
DAYA.   O stop, look here!
NATHAN. In dying now he lacks for comfort, all—
  Except awareness of his deed.
DAYA.   Stop, stop!
  You're killing her!
NATHAN.   And you have murdered him!—
  You could have killed him so.—Come, Rachel, Rachel!
  It's medicine, not poison, that I give.
  He lives!—Recover!—nor is sick, I think;
  Not even sick!
RACHEL.   For sure?—not dead? not sick?
NATHAN. For sure, not dead!—For God rewards good deeds,
  Done here, among us.—Go!—But see how far
  It's easier to swoon in pious dreams
  Than do good actions? see how sluggish men
  Are fond of dreaming piously, because—
  Although at times of their intent not quite
  Aware—they'd shun the need of doing good?

One clearly feels that Lessing belongs to the pedagogical century, the century that also produced a Rousseau and a Pestalozzi. Not only does Nathan get his daughter to think for herself step by step, so that she must believe her own conclusions; at the same time, he engages her lively imagination and uses it for his own purposes. This same imagination that was so zealous in fabricating the miracle involving the angel is now engaged in imbuing the idea that her resuer might be ill with reality. Rachel is healed, her tendency to believe in astonishing miracles and to dream of them is overcome, and she resigns herself to thinking humbly and sensibly about reality and to acting in accordance with her responsibility.

This humble awareness that even ordinary existence—the things of nature which lie before us—is full of secrets and wonders, brought forth its finest fruits in the eighteenth and nineteenth centuries in life, science, and literature. "From the life-giving sun to the smallest plant, everything is a miracle," said the poet Salomon Gessner. And another Zürich poet, Johann Caspar Lavater, who called man "the greatest and most incomprehensible miracle in nature," contrasted the two views eloquently: "To subsist forty days without food or drink is a divine miracle; but it is also a miracle to live on food and drink for forty years." The Hamburg poet Barthold Heinrich Brockes called the world:

> A book in which we perceive the true God,
> O wonder! here one can read the writing of God's being
> Not only with the eyes, but with all the senses.
> O mysterious book, O spelling book of miracles
> In which I am both reader and letter!

Klopstock rhapsodizes: "All around me is omnipotence and miracle! With deep reverence I gaze at creation." These are voices of the eighteenth century. The definitive statement was made in the nineteenth century by Adalbert Stifter without making use of the word "miracle." Behind the contrast of miracle and nature is the more common one of outstanding and incon-

spicuous, extraordinary and common, great and small. states in his preface to *Bunte Steine* (Colorful Stones):

> The stirring of the wind, the trickling of the water, the ing of the grain, the rolling of the sea, the greening of the eart radiance of the heavens and the glimmering of the stars—th consider great. The thunder storm that advances with pomp splendor, the bolt of lightning that cleaves houses, the storm drives the pounding surf, the mountain spewing forth fire and earthquake that leaves whole countries buried in rubble—the consider no greater than the former phenomena: indeed I cons them as lesser, because they are only the consequences of m higher laws. They occur in scattered locations and are the result one-sided causes. The force which makes the milk rise up and o flow in the poor woman's saucepan is the same as the one wh drives up the lava within a volcano and spews forth the molt material which then flows down the slopes of the mountains. T latter phenomena are only more conspicuous and attract mo attention from those who are unknowledgeable and inattentiv whereas the scientist directs his attention primarily to the totali and what is generally true and only in it perceives the sublime because it alone is what sustains the world.

Adalbert Stifter, who has been called the poet of reverence never tired of portraying the silent wonders of nature and of human relationships as purely as possible, without tampering with them or trying to make them something they were not. It is, perhaps, the most characteristic accomplishment of literature in the nineteenth century that it plainly and reverently perceived and celebrated the things of this world, and specifically that which is insignificant and common. Goethe had demonstrated very early in his *Hermann und Dorothea* (1797) that the small town and ordinary citizen was as worthy as the noble heroes of Homer of being celebrated in hexameters. In place of the poetic emotion brought about by the miracle in the saint's legend, fairy tale, or heroic myth, there now appears the sense for the miracle of the confrontation—with other men, with nature, or with fate.

Parallel with this entire development, verse recedes more and

> To the succeeding royalty he leaves
> The healing benediction. With this strange virtue,
> He hath a heavenly gift of prophecy,
> And sundry blessings hang about his throne,
> That speak him full of grace.

A doctor and a king's son thus portray the king of England and the miracles he performs in healing the incurably sick by merely touching them. Here we come upon an element which seems inseparably bound up with the Christian concept of the miracle. The vast majority of the miracles of Christ that have been handed down concern the curing of the sick. Here, the miracle is not only a demonstration of divine power, it is called upon to bring redemption. The healing powers of the English ruler legitimate him as a genuine king. In former times, the king and the priest were the same person: the medieval king, like the priest, took both the bread and wine of communion, and the golden crown is reminiscent of the golden halo surrounding the heads of the saints. The genuine king can be a savior to his people. That the king of England cures the sick is a vivid symbol for the fact that he is also called on to cure the wounds of his country, whereas Macbeth only inflicts harm on his own. And the assertion that the English king's healing power shall be handed down to his successors shows its fundamental significance: it is not his as an individual, but in his position as king. Thus, from the conversation between the doctor and the prince there emerges the true picture of the king in contrast to the egomaniacal Macbeth, who murders instead of healing, who destroys instead of building and ordering, who plunges his realm into chaos and finally perishes in the chaos himself. Macbeth's terrible fury dominates the stage, whereas the image of the healing, saintly king arises only in the mind of the hearer, for he is only spoken of and does not appear. But this is just what gives him a special radiance. The miracle has its origin in another world, and Shakespeare lets it take place beyond the stage. The scenic portrayal would not have presented the slightest problem, but the great poet preferred merely to evoke it in the mind of the viewer and not present it physically on the stage. The figures of the genuine king, had it been materialized and brought before the public, would not have the brilliance that it can achieve in the imagination of the listener. The image of the wonder-working English king, sketched in a few strokes and arising only in the mind of the audience, has the effect of a light in the darkness of this turbulent drama.

Lux in tenebris is the essence of the miracle in the world. It lives in the minds of the common folk and of the poets as a light in darkness. Why do we light candles on Christmas Eve? Because we sense the light as a symbol of the miracle that occurred on that night. Gottfried Keller writes:

> *It was a Christmas tree glimmering with candles*
> *I still see it shimmering before me in its beauty,*
> *The green miracle in the brightened room.*

Symbolism involving light is found in the religions and literatures of all peoples. To the mystics, God repeatedly appeared as light. And when we today use the word "miracle," we automatically think of the appearance of divine light.

The struggle against the craving for visible miracles begins as early as the New Testament. The famous statement of Jesus is found in the Gospel according to St. John (4:48): "Unless you see signs and wonders you will not believe." And yet at the very moment He is speaking, He cures the deathly ill son of the official from Capernaum. The miracle as proof of power is rejected here —the real significance of the miracle is now the act of healing. In literature of more modern times the saving, healing act is entrusted to man. "Do I summon the goddess for a miracle?" asks the title heroine of Goethe's *Iphigenia* in her great confusion. But she continues: "Is there no strength in the depths of my soul?" The drama portrays the transition from a childlike existence dominated by miracles to confidence in the miraculous strength which God has placed in the heart of man. Iphigenia, while still a helpless child, was about to be sacrificed when a goddess saved her through a miracle. The grownup Iphigenia can no longer let herself be saved in this way—now she must perform the miracle herself. In venturing to do the apparently impossible, she saves not only herself and her brother, she also saves the image of the gods in her own soul and in that of the barbarians. "Not yet have I my liberty made good," says Faust (in the Bayard Taylor translation) at the end of his life. (*Faust,* II, act V, scene 5)

> *If I could banish Magic's fell creations,*
> *And totally unlearn the incantations,—*
> *Stood I, O Nature! Man alone in thee,*
> *Then were it worth one's while a man to be!*

And in Gerhart Hauptmann's *Emanuel Quint,* we read, "The miracle worker is a perpetrator of violence." From the eighteenth century on into the twentieth, the struggle was waged against the miracle, regarded as an external act of violence. However, the miracle as the appearance of light continued to be celebrated. Iphigenia, too, is a bringer of light; the miracle of her existence and her decision is able to heal the world. Healing, change, transformation, resurrection—these things are at the heart of the miracle.

In spite of the great influence of the Enlightenment, poets and their readers have retained an appreciation for the poetic charm of the miracle. Despite the beauty of Stifter's veneration of nature and despite the fact that the satisfaction with a realistic portrayal of this world can be a splendid thing, it would indeed be an impoverishment if what is unusal, beyond reality, miraculous, should completely disappear from literature. For the Romantics, that "which raises us above ordinary reality into a world of the imagination" was the very essence of the poetic. In our time, Friedrich Dürrenmatt proclaims, "Reality in the theater must be balanced with something above and beyond reality." And, indeed, one cannot say that literature in the twentieth century is antipathetic toward what is fantastic, fabulous, and miraculous. The miracle, though not accepted as real, has become an image and appears in many forms, even though it may be disguised in the form of the absurd or the incomprehensible. To the Romantics, the wondrous blue flower was a symbol for the fact that

darkness can unite with light and that the earthly can be wedded
to the divine. The meeting of earthly darkness and divine light—
this is what occurs in the miracle and this is what the Romantics
and poets generally never tire of describing.

Romanticism, some features of which are picked up again
and continued in modern literature, was not only fascinated by
the fairy tale and miracles; it also delighted in toying with the
miracle and the miraculous. Thus, at the conclusion of our series
of essays, let us recall to mind Chamisso's *The Wonderful History
of Peter Schlemihl,* in which the hero sells his shadow. The
author unforgettably portrays the moment in which the shadow is
miraculously separated from the body. As compensation for the
shadow, the buyer, a modest plain-looking man in a grey suit,
offers the astonished Schlemihl the wishing purse of Fortunatus.

> "Would it please my Lord to examine this purse and try it?"
> He put his hand in his pocket and pulled out the purse by its two
> stout leather laces and handed it to me. It was made of Cordovan
> leather, rather large and tightly stitched. I reached in and pulled
> out ten gold pieces and, repeating this action, ten more, and ten
> more and ten more! I quickly held out my hand—"Agreed! It's a
> deal; for the purse you have my shadow!" He shook hands and
> forthwith knelt down in front of me. As I watched he gently and
> with great skill detached my shadow from the grass, from my head
> to my feet, then lifted it up, rolled and folded it together and
> finally put it in his pocket. He arose, bowed to me again and with-
> drew in the direction of the rose bush. It seemed to me I heard him
> laughing quietly to himself, but I held the purse firmly by its laces.
> All around me the world was sunny and bright and I had not yet
> come to my senses.

"I had not yet come to my senses," says Peter Schlemihl, and
earlier he said, "I became dizzy and there was a glittering and
flickering as of golden doubloons before my eyes." Here, the
miracle is not enlightening but benumbing and bewildering. It is
not a divine but a satanic miracle, not white magic but black
magic—although, in the glimmering of the doubloons, there is
still a dim reminder of the fact that Lucifer, too, was originally a

bearer of light. *The Wonderful History of Peter Schlemihl* describes how the unsuspecting hero (a predecessor of the modern negative hero) succumbs to the seduction of the evil one. Why shouldn't one give up his shadow—which, after all, is not his *soul*—if he can get in return an inexhaustible purse of gold? After all, all kinds of good and sensible things could be done with the money, whereas the shadow is an unsubstantial and inconsequential thing. But Schlemihl will have to learn by experience that people reject anyone who is different from themselves, even if it is in such an insignificant respect as a shadow. He finally resigns himself to this, but he no longer wants to keep the miraculous purse, which, as he now knows, was given to him by the devil. He casts it away and, with the last gold pieces, buys a pair of old shoes. These unexpectedly turn out to be seven-league boots, which carry him effortlessly to distant parts of the world. Thus, at the very moment he renounces the satanic miracle of the purse of gold, Schlemihl is given the opportunity to search out and study the miracles of earthly nature in all parts of the world. The dreamer turns into an explorer and researcher. Chamisso leads his hero away from his daydreaming to a reality full of miracles, and in this respect is a remote descendant of Lessing. But, unlike Lessing, he does it with the help of another fantastic image: the fabulous boots which carry Peter Schlemihl out of the world of daydreams and miracles and into the world of divinely created nature. "All around me the world was sunny and bright," it reads at the very beginning of the process, but only much later does Schlemihl learn to appreciate the miracles of the sun-filled world, even though he must venture forth into this bright sun without a shadow. Thus, in *The Wonderful History of Peter Schlemihl* there is an overcoming of the fairy tale by the fairy tale and an overcoming of the miracle by the miracle, as a visible sign that both remain indispensable for the poet.

REFERENCE NOTES

(*Ed. note:* The most complete listing of bibliographical references is carried under Chapter 10 in this section.)

CHAPTER 1 SLEEPING BEAUTY

1. Fritz Ernst, *Dornröschen in drei Sprachen,* Bern 1949, contains the texts of Basile (in the original and in German translation), Perrault, and Grimm (in the editions of 1812 and 1819), as well as an introduction by the editor.
2. Hedwig von Beit, *Symbolik des Märchens,* (2nd ed.), Bern 1960, gives a Jungian interpretation of Grimm's "Sleeping Beauty" (pp. 695–701).
3. Jan de Vries, *"Dornröschen,"* in *Fabula* 2 (Berlin 1958), pp. 110–121, examines the early history of the fairy tale, tracing it back to a medieval French tale. With regard to the motif of the "suckling finger"—found as early as the fourteenth century in *Perceforest,* a French romance in prose—see also, Albert Wesselski, *Erlesenes,* Prague 1928, pp. 144–150.
4. Friedrich von der Leyen and Kurt Schier, *Das Märchen,* Heidelberg 1958. Taking *"Dornröschen"* as an example, the authors briefly demonstrate the procedures used by various schools of thought in the interpretation of a fairy tale (pp. 23–26).

5. Karl Justus Obenauer, *Das Märchen, Dichtung und Deutung*, Frankfurt a.M. 1959, (pp. 54–67).
6. For older literature, see Johannes Bolte and Georg Polívka, *Anmerkungen zu den Kinder- und Hausmärchen der Brüder Grimm*, vol. 1, Leipzig 1913–1932, pp. 434–442; and the *Handwörterbuch des deutschen Märchens*, vol. 1, Berlin 1930–1940. Basile's tale is taken from the German version of Felix Liebrecht (1846, reprinted 1928).

Additional notes by Utley:

   "Sleeping Beauty" is Tale Type. 410, and in many ways is the masculine-centered version of Type 425, Cupid and Psyche, in which the disenchantment is by the act of the heroine. See Stith Thompson, *The Folktale*, (2nd ed.), New York 1953, pp. 96–98. For English versions, see N. M. Penzer, ed., *The Pentamerone of Giambattista Basile*, London 1932, tales ii. 8 and v. 5. This edition has valuable essays on the history and nature of the folk tale by Benedetto Croce and Stith Thompson.

CHAPTER 2   THE SEVEN SLEEPERS

On the saint's legend:

1. Hellmut Rosenfeld, *Legende*, (2nd ed.), Stuttgart 1964.
2. André Jolles, "Legende," in *Einfache Formen*, Halle 1930 (reprinted Tübingen, 1965).

On the local legend and fairy tale:

3. Max Lüthi, *Volksmärchen und Volkssage, zwei Grundformen erzählender Dichtung*, Bern 1961.
4. ———, *Die Gabe im Märchen und in der Sage*, dissertation, Bern 1943.
5. P. Michael Huber, *Die Wanderlegende von den Siebenschläfern*, Leipzig 1910, discusses the motif of various figures who sleep a long time, among them the Seven Sleepers, Evo, the Monk of Heisterbach, Monk Felix, and Rip van Winkle.
6. Fritz Müller, *Die Legende vom verzückten Mönch*, dissertation, Erlangen 1913.
7. Karl Meisen, "*Der in den Himmel entrückte Bräutigam*," in *Rheinisches Jahrbuch für Volkskunde*, vol. 6, Bonn 1955, pp. 118-175.
8. Lutz Röhrich, "*Der entrückte Mönch*," in *Erzählungen des späten Mittelalters und ihr Weiterleben in Literatur und Volksdichtung bis zur Gegenwart*, vol. 1, Bern and Munich, 1962.

Reference Notes

9. The tale of the Seven Sleepers is reproduced here according to Jacobus a Voragine, *Legenda Aurea* in the German translation by Richard Benz, vol. 1, Leipzig 1917 (reprinted in Heidelberg, no date); the tale about Prior Evo is taken from Johannes Jegerlehner, *Sagen und Märchen aus dem Oberwallis,* Basel 1913; and the legend of Abbot Erpho comes from Paul Zaunert, *Rheinland-Sagen,* vol. 1, Jena 1924. The Breton tale ("The Crystal Palace") can be found in Ré Soupault, *Bretonische Märchen,* Düsseldorf and Cologne, 1959 (in the series *Märchen der Weltliteratur*).

Additional notes by Utley:

On the sleepers of both the first and second chapters, see the essay on "The Supernatural Lapse of Time in Fairyland," in E. S. Hartland, *Science of Fairy Tales,* London 1891, pp. 160–254. For "The Seven Sleepers," see Herbert Thurston and Donald Attwater, eds., *Butler's Lives of the Saints,* vol. 3, London 1956, pp. 193–196. They were celebrated also among the Moslems; see Francis L. Utley, "Rabghuzi—Fourteenth-Century Turkic Folklorist," in *Volksüberlieferung: Festschrift für Kurt Ranke,* Göttingen 1968, pp. 373–400. All Americans will think of Washington Irving's "Rip Van Winkle," from *The Sketch Book,* New York 1819–1820; it is adapted from Otmar (Johann Carl Cristoph Nachtigall), *Volcs-Sagen,* Bremen 1800. For a translation of the German, see Thomas Roscoe, *The German Novelists,* vol. 2, London 1826, pp. 47–60. The changes for local color are most interesting. The best study of saints' legends in English goes by that title, and was written by Gordon Hall Gerould, Boston 1916. Consult also the works of Hippolyte Delahaye, some of which have been translated into English. For a basic bibliography, see Robert E. Spiller and others, *Literary History of the United States,* New York, 1948, bibliography, pp. 578–583.

CHAPTER 3 THE DRAGON SLAYER

1. Kurt Ranke, *Die Zwei Brüder. Eine Studie zur vergleichenden Märchenforschung,* Helsinki 1934.
2. Heino Gehrts, *Das Märchen und das Opfer. Unterschungen zum europäischen Brüdermärchen,* Bonn 1967.
3. Max Lüthi, *Volksmärchen und Volkssage, op. cit.*
4. The Swedish fairy tale appears in *Europäische Volksmärchen* (Manesse) and in *Nordische Volksmärchen,* vol. 1 (*Märchen der Weltliteratur*).

The Austrian tale is found in Paul Zaunert, *Märchen aus dem Donaulande (M.d.W.)* and Karl Haiding, *Österreichs Märchenschatz.* The Breton phrases appear in Ré Soupault, *Bretonische Märchen (M.d.W.).*

Additional notes by Utley:

For "The Two Brothers", see Tale Type 303, and for "The Dragon Slayer," Type 300. See Thompson, *op. cit.,* pp. 24–33. The Egyptian tale of "The Two Brothers," often called the oldest fairy tale in the world, will be found in James B. Pritchard, *Ancient Near Eastern Texts Relating to the Old Testament,* Princeton 1950, pp. 23–25. It is closely related to the Joseph and Potiphar's wife episode in the Bible. For the relationship of "The Dragon Slayer" to the *Odyssey,* see Rhys Carpenter, *Folktale, Fiction and Saga in the Homeric Epics,* Berkeley and Los Angeles 1946. For a similar relationship to *Beowulf,* see R. W. Chambers, *Beowulf: An Introduction,* Cambridge, England 1932. On the modern structural approach (binary and polarized) to anthropology and folklore, see John Middleton, ed., *Myth and Cosmos,* New York 1967; Alan Dundes, *The Morphology of North American Indian Folktales,* Helsinki 1964; Vladimir Propp, *Morphology of the Folk Tale,* Bloomington 1958; Claude Lévi-Strauss, *Structural Anthropology,* New York 1963.

CHAPTER 4   THE USES OF THE FAIRY TALE

For Cinderella, see next chapter's listing. For the German variant in Hungary, see Elli Zenker-Starzacher, *Eine deutsche Märchenerzählerin aus Ungarn,* Munich 1941.

For Hansel and Gretel (Type 327A), see Thompson, *op. cit.,* pp. 36–37. Also, Bolte and Polívka, *op. cit.,* vol. 1, p. 115. See, too, Hans Traxler, *Die Wahrheit über Hänsel und Gretel,* Frankfurt a.M. 1963.

"The White Snake" is Type 673; see Thompson, *op. cit.,* pp. 83–85, where other animal-language stories are discussed, and Bolte and Polívka, *op. cit.,* vol. 1, p. 131.

CHAPTER 5   THE LITTLE EARTH-COW

1. "The Little Earth-Cow" in Albert Wesselski, *Deutsche Märchen vor Grimm,* Brünn and Leipzig 1938; also, in Ninon Hesse, *Deutsche*

Märchen vor und nach Grimm, Zürich 1956 (Commentary by Ninon Hesse in the *"Neue Zürcher Zeitung,"* April 3, 1960.) The original text of the tale is entitled *"Ein schön History von einer Frawen mit zweyen Kindlin,"* in Martin Montanus, *Ander theyl der Gartengesellschaft,* Strassburg circa 1560. The Lotharingian fairy tale (*"Der wundersame Hirsch"*) appears in Angelika Merkelback-Pinck, *Lothringer Volksmärchen,* Düsseldorf and Cologne, 1961 (*M.d.W.*). The group of Cinderella tales, to which "The Little Earth Cow" belongs, is discussed in Anna Birgitta Rooth, *The Cinderella Cycle,* Lund 1951.

Additional notes by Utley:
See Thompson, *op.cit.,* pp. 126–129 (Types 510, 510A, 511, 511A).

CHAPTER 6 THE LIVING DOLL

1. Max Lüthi, *"Gattungsstile,"* in *Volksmärchen und Volkssage, op. cit.*
2. The tale from Uri appears in Josef Müller, *Sagen aus Uri,* vol. 2, Basel 1929; the Greek fairy tale is taken from Irene Naumann-Mavrogordato, *Es war einmal, Neugriechische Volksmärchen,* Istanbul 1942. There are similar texts in Paul Kretzschmer, *Neugriechische Märchen, (M.d.W.),* and in N.M. Penzer, *op. cit.,* vol. 2, pp. 114–119. The iron shoes with which the princess travels to other worlds (a frequent motif in folk fairy tales), when viewed historically, call to mind shoes found placed in graves for the benefit of the deceased; similarly, the man of groats or sugar is suggestive of wax figures made in the Middle Ages that were supposed to give one magical power over a beloved. Within the fairy tale, this man of sugar or groats is an unusual, mysterious type of supernatural spouse. The beast-bridegroom who appeared to the heroine was a representative of another world; but here, the princess creates the supernatural creature and marries her self-made charm. See also the Italian, Greek, and Turkish fairy tales in which a girl, or a childless woman, creates a baby out of dough or wood, which is then brought to life by fairies, the Fatal Sisters, or a dervish; also, Ovid's tale about Pygmalion, who fell in love with an ivory statue he had made, and married it after Aphrodite, at his request, had brought it to life (Metamorphoses 10).

Additional notes by Utley:

Pintosmalto and the Sugar-Man tales are special versions of the famous Monstrous-Bridegroom story, Type 425, on which see San-Öjvind Swahn, *The Tale of Cupid and Psyche,* Lund 1955. They are thus remotely related to the tale of Griselda, which attracted the talents of Boccaccio, Petrarch, and Chaucer. See Dudley D. Griffith, *The Origin of the Griselda Story,* Seattle 1931, and the Chaucer bibliographies. A Greek version will be found in R. M. Dawkins, *Forty-five Stories from the Dodekanese,* Cambridge, England 1950, pp. 105–114.

The question of the classification of the local legend or *Sage* is now being much debated. See Fourth International Congress for Folk Narrative Research in Athens: Lectures and Reports, Åthens 1965 (the same as Laographia XXII); see especially the essay on "Processes of Legend Formation" by Linda Dégh, pp. 76–87.

CHAPTER 7   ANIMAL STORIES

1. The Indian tales in Theodor Koch-Grünberg, *Indianermärchen aus Südamerika (M.d.W.)*; the African tale in Carl Meinhof, *Afrikanische Märchen (M.d.W.)*. See also the other non-European volumes of the *Märchen der Weltliteratur* and of the collection *Das Gesicht der Völker.*

Additional notes by Utley:

For the animal tales of the American Negro, in a literary version, see Joel Chandler Harris, *The Complete Tales of Uncle Remus,* Richard Chase, ed., Boston 1955. On the American Indian, see Stith Thompson, *Tales of the North American Indian,* Cambridge, Mass. 1929. For Aesop, see R. T. Lenaghan, ed., Caxton's *Aesop,* Cambridge, Mass. 1967; and the invaluable Ben Edwin Perry, ed., Loeb Classic *Babrius and Phaedrus,* Cambridge, Mass. 1965, with an appendix which lists all the fable collections and their parallels. A translation of both French and Flemish versions of Renard the Fox is much needed in English; for the moment, we must be content with the reprint of Caxton's (1481) truncated version of the Flemish: Donald B. Sands, ed., *The History of Reynard the Fox,* Cambridge, Mass. 1960. See the splendid study of English painting and woodcarving, Kenneth Varty, *Reynard the Fox,* Leicester 1967. For aboriginal literature in general, see John Greenway,

The Primitive Reader, Hatboro, Penna. 1965, and his *Literature among the Primitives,* Hatboro, Penna. 1964.

CHAPTER 8   RAPUNZEL

1. Max Lüthi, "Rapunzel," in *Volksmärchen und Volkssage, op. cit.*
2. Josephine Bilz, *"Märchengeschehen und Reifungsvorgänge unter tiefenpsychologischem Gesichtspunkt,"* in C. Bühler and J. Bilz, *Das Märchen und die Phantasie des Kindes,* (2nd ed.), Munich 1961.
3. Walter Scherf, *Kindermärchen in dieser Zeit?,* Munich 1961.
4. ———, *"Was bedeutet dem Kind die Grausamkeit der Volksmärchen?,"* in *Jugendliteratur,* 1960.
5. The Grimm Brothers' first version of "Rapunzel" is reproduced in Friedrich Panzer, *Die Kinder- und Hausmärchen der Brüder Grimm in ihrer Urgestalt,* vol. 1, Hamburg 1948. The Maltese tales appear in Bertha Ilg, *Maltesische Märchen und Schwänke,* vol. 1, Hannover, 1909; the Italian tale in Antonio De Nino, *Usi e costumi Abruzzesi,* vol. 3, Florence 1883; and in the *Archivio per lo Studio Delle Tradizioni Popolari,* vol. 1, Palermo 1882; the French tale in Paul Delarue, *Le conte populaire francais,* vol. 1, Paris 1957.

Additional notes by Utley:

"Rapunzel" is Tale Type 310, or The Maiden in the Tower. For an Italian version, see Thompson, *The Folktale, op. cit.,* pp. 102–103. Penzer, *op. cit.,* vol. 1, pp. 135–140 ("Petrosinella"). For the deluding of the spying parrot, see Chaucer's "Manciple's Tale" (Type 1422).

The ceremonial aspects of maturation or initiation have long attracted the attention of anthropologists and literary students. See Arnold van Gennep, *The Rites of Passage,* Chicago 1960; Mircea Eliade, *Birth and Rebirth,* New York 1958; Francis L. Utley, Lynn Z. Bloom, and Arthur F. Kinney, *Bear, Man and God,* New York 1964.

CHAPTER 9   THE RIDDLE PRINCESS

1. Jan de Vries, *Die Märchen von klugen Rätsellösern,* Helsinki 1928.
2. Albert Wesselski, *"Der Knabenkönig und das kluge Mädchen,"* Sudetendeutsche Zeitschrift für Volkskunde,* Prague 1929, supplement 1.
3. Walter Anderson, *Kaiser und Abt, Die Geschichte eines Schwanks,* Helsinki 1923.

4. Lutz Röhrich, *"Der Kaiser und der Abt"* and *"Dummling und Prinzessin im Redewettkampf,"* in *Erzählungen des späten Mittelalters* . . . , Bern and Munich 1962.
5. The modern Greek fairy tale is found in I. Naumann, *Es war einmal,* Istanbul 1942; the Persian tale (Turandot) in *Tausendundein Tag,* vol. 1, Leipzig 1925; the Breton tale in *Europäische Volksmärchen* (Manesse).

Additional notes by Utley:

The riddle is also well known in the ballad literature. See Francis James Child, *The English and Scottish Popular Ballads,* vol. 1, New York 1956, pp. 1–6, 414–425 (Nos. 1, 46); and on riddles in general, Archer Taylor's two books, *The Literary Riddle before 1600,* Berkeley and Los Angeles 1948, and *English Riddles from Oral Tradition,* Berkeley and Los Angeles 1951. In Tale Type 1178, the devil is outwitted by a riddling boy; in Type 927, a judge is outriddled by so-called "neck riddles," in which the answer is a personal one; in Types 851 and 851a, a princess is won by a riddle (the last is Turandot); in Type 875, the riddle solver is a clever peasant girl who wins the king as husband; and in Type 922, emperor and abbot, a clever shepherd saves his master by his answers to the king's riddles. On cleverness and riddle-solving in general, including all these tales, see Thompson, *The Folktale,* pp. 152–165.

Translations for the Schiller extracts were done by Charles E. Passage.

CHAPTER 10   THE FAIRY-TALE HERO

A selected bibliography of general literature on the folk fairy tale:

Reference works:

1. Johannes Bolte and Georg Polívka, *op. cit.*
2. *Handwörterbuch des deutschen Märchens, op. cit.* (This unfinished work is to be superseded in a few years by an international encyclopedia of the fairy tale).
3. Waldemar Liungman, *Die schwedischen Volksmärchen. Herkunft und Geschichte,* Berlin 1961.
4. Antti Aarne and Stith Thompson, *The Types of the Folktale,* (3d ed.), Helsinki 1961.

5. Stith Thompson, *Motif-Index of Folk-Literature,* (2nd ed.), Copenhagen 1955–1958.

Descriptive works:

6. Friedrich von der Leyen, *Das Märchen. Ein Versuch,* (4th ed.), Munich 1958.
7. ———, *Die Welt der Märchen,* Düsseldorf, 1953, 1954.
8. Max Lüthi, *Das europäische Volksmärchen. Form und Wesen,* (3rd ed.), Bern and Munich 1968.
9. ———, *Märchen,* (3rd ed.), Stuttgart 1968.
10. ———, *Volksmärchen und Volkssage, op. cit.*
11. Karl Justus Obenauer, *op. cit.*
12. Jan de Vries, *Betrachtungen zum Märchen, besonders in seinem Verhältnis zu Heldensage und Mythos,* Helsinki 1954.
13. Lutz Röhrich, *Märchen und Wirklichkeit,* (2nd ed.), Wiesbaden 1964.
14. Stith Thompson, *The Folktale, op. cit.*
15. Roger Pinon, *Le Conte merveilleux comme sujet d'Etudes,* Liège 1955.
16. Hedwig von Beit, *op. cit.*
17. ———, *Das Märchen. Sein Ort in der geistigen Entwicklung,* Bern and Munich 1965.

Collections:

18. *Die Märchen der Weltliteratur (M.d.W.),* formerly Jena, now Düsseldorf and Cologne 1912.
19. *Das Gesicht der Völker,* Eisenach and Kassel 1952.
20. *Märchen der europäischen Völker, Märchen aus deutschen Landschaften, Begegnung der Völker im Märchen,* Münster 1961.
21. Fairy-tale texts of the *Fabula* series, Berlin 1959.

Additional notes by Utley:

The two best English translations of *Grimm's Household Tales* are by Margaret Hunt and by Magoun and Krappe. In English, the best series of authentic folk-tale texts is Richard M. Dorson, ed., *Folktales of the World,* Chicago 1963. There are, so far, volumes for Japan, France, Germany, Hungary, England, Norway, China, and Chile. The great nineteenth-century collection, *Les littératures populaires de toutes les nations,* is being reprinted by G.-P. Maisonneuve and Larose of Paris. Laurits Bødker *et al., European Folk Tales,* Copenhagen 1963, is a collection of accurately recorded tales from Western Europe, with a historical

introduction on the folk tale. The fullest account in English of the historical method is Stith Thompson, *The Folktale, op. cit.* E. S. Hartland,
The Science of Fairy Tales, op. cit., is old fashioned but full of valuable
comparative data. W. A. Clouston, *Popular Tales and Fictions,* Edinburg
and London 1887, is a pioneer study of tales in English, now much outmoded because of its confusion of tale types and motifs or simple narrative elements. It is still useful for single tales. Alexander Haggerty
Krappe, *The Science of Folk-Lore,* London 1930, is somewhat eccentric,
but the best survey in English of the various genres of folk literature.

Some special American books to be studied by those wishing to
proceed from our own folklore: Ernest W. Baughman, *Type and Motif
Index of the Folktales of England and North America,* The Hague 1966.
Richard M. Dorson, *Negro Folktales in Michigan,* Cambridge, Mass.
1956, and *Negro Tales from Pine Bluff, Arkansas, and Calvin, Michigan,*
Bloomington 1958 (recently joined together in a paperback, *Negro Folk-
tales in America*). Bruce Jackson, ed., *The Negro and His Folklore in
Nineteenth-Century Periodicals,* Austin Tex. 1967. Tristram P. Coffin,
Our Living Traditions: An Introduction to American Folklore, New
York 1968 (lectures by a number of American scholars for Voice of
America broadcasts).

Works on folk-tale theory are rare in English. Besides Thompson's
The Folktale and the structural studies mentioned in the bibliography to
Chapter 3, see Emma Emily Kiefer, *Albert Wesselski and Recent Folktale
Theories,* Bloomington 1947 and C. W. von Sydow, *Selected Papers on
Folklore,* Copenhagen 1948. See also Alan Dundes, ed., *The Study of
Folklore,* New York 1965.

CHAPTER 11   THE MIRACLE IN LITERATURE

1. The article *Wunder* in the *Deutsches Wörterbuch* (begun by Jacob
   and Wilhelm Grimm), vol. 14, cols. 1782–1824.

INDEX